PC Publishing

R A Penfold

Synthesizers for musicians
Get the best from your synth or sampler

PC Publishing
4 Brook Street
Tonbridge
Kent TN9 2PJ

First published 1989

© PC Publishing 1989

ISBN 1 870775 01 5

British Library Cataloguing in Publication Data

Penfold, R.A.
  Synthesizers for musicians.
  1. Musical instruments : Synthesizers
  I. Title
  789.9'9

  ISBN 1–870775–01–5

Phototypesetting by Scribe Design, Gillingham, Kent
Printed and bound by LR Printing Services, Manor Royal, Crawley, West Sussex

Synthesizers for musicians

Preface

In the past, synthesizers have been relatively crude instruments which were capable of an unrivaled range of sounds, but lacked polyphony (the ability to play more than one note at a time) and were not usually touch sensitive. Synthesizers have now come of age, and their sounds and range of features are second to none in the music world. Just one modern synthesizer can sound like a whole bank of instruments playing. A good synthesizer can put as much expression into the music as its player is capable of providing.

The problem with the power and versatility of modern synthesizers is that they require a degree of learning effort from the user if they are to be fully mastered. You can simply use the manufacturer's preset sounds, or adopt a process of random 'twiddling', but with a basic knowledge of the nature of sound and sound synthesis techniques you can go so much further than this.

With the aid of this book you should be able to understand the make-up of various sounds, all the major methods of sound synthesis (including sampling), and how to pair these two sets of knowledge so that you can produce the sounds you require. Provided you have a good ear for music the art of sound synthesis is much easier than you might think.

Contents

6 Effects units   **129**

Delay; Digital delay; Bucket brigades; Chorus; Phasing;
Flanging; Reverberation; In the mix; The rest.

1 Introduction to sound

In the early days, synthesizers were very much a minority interest and had something of an avant garde image. This situation gradually changed, with synthesizers being regarded more as the tools of professional rock and pop musicians. Pianos, organs and portable keyboards are probably still more popular amongst home users, but synthesizers are beginning to make definite inroads into this part of the musical instrument market. One reason for this is that people tend to be less intimidated by technology than was once the case. Probably a larger factor is that synthesizers have improved dramatically in recent years, while prices have remained virtually constant (and have fallen in 'real terms'). Now a few hundred pounds can buy you a five octave, eight note polyphonic instrument with a long list of useful features.

A lot of musicians are attracted by the power of modern synthesizers, but are put off by the unfamiliar terminology and techniques. Some buy synthesizers but use only the factory preset sounds. While a synthesizer has tremendous music making potential when used in this way, I can not help thinking that this is like buying a box of paints and never bothering to mix them to obtain the exact colours you require. Synthesizers are complex pieces of electronics, but with a little effort they can be mastered by anyone who is reasonably musical. The gateway to their full palette of sounds is then opened up.

Pressure and sound

If you are to stand a reasonable chance of mastering sound synthesis, one prerequisite is an understanding of the nature of sound. Without knowing at least a few of the basics, the standard methods of sound synthesis can not be properly mastered. You may be able to get the sounds you require using 'hit and miss' methods, but a logical approach based on a proper understanding of the subject will almost invariably provide better results much more quickly.

1

Looking at things in the most basic possible terms, objects that vibrate in air produce sound waves, which are increases and decreases in the air pressure. As the object moves forward it compresses the air to give increased pressure. As it moves backwards it rarefies the air and produces decreased pressure. These changes in pressure spread out in a wave-like manner, and at over 1000 kilometres per hour. The greater the changes in pressure, the louder the sound. The more rapid the changes, the higher the pitch of the sound they carry.

Pitch

The pitch, or 'frequency' of a sound as it is more usually termed in technical circles, is measured in hertz. A sound at one hertz has one complete cycle (i.e. a rise in pressure, a fall in pressure, and a return to the original pressure value) per second. The audio frequency range is normally given as extending from 20 hertz to 20000 hertz. High frequencies such as 20000 hertz are usually stated in kilohertz, and one kilohertz = 1000 hertz. This sets the upper limit of the audio range as 20 kilohertz (or just 20kHz for short).

There are no strict limits on the audio range, as some people can perceive a much wider range of frequencies than others. Generally people in their teens have optimum hearing with regard to frequency response, and they may well be able to hear the full 20Hz to 20kHz range, or something approaching it. Someone who has spent a lot of time in a very noisy environment is likely to have

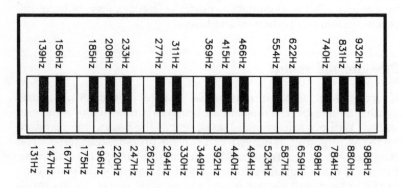

Figure 1.1 Frequencies for a range of notes (440Hz is middle A)

suffered some damage to their hearing, and might only be able to hear properly over a very restricted range of frequencies.

In the past there have been several standards for the pitch of musical notes, but these days the so-called 'concert pitch' seems to be the widely accepted standard, and this has middle A at a pitch of 440Hz. The keyboard diagram of Fig.1.1 shows a range of notes and their standard pitches in hertz. Remember that going up an octave is a doubling of frequency, going down an octave is a halving of frequency. With a little mathematics you can therefore work out the frequency of any musical note from the example frequencies provided in Fig.1.1.

Equal temperament

Since the days of Bach we have used the tempered scale, or equal tempered as it is also known. This has each semitone at a frequency which is 1.05946 times the frequency of the semitone below it. There are twelve semitone increments in an octave, and multiplying 440Hz by 1.05946, then multiplying the answer by this figure, and repeating the process a further ten times should give an answer of 880Hz (running this calculation on a computer I obtained a result of 879.9697Hz, which is near enough!). The main point about this scale is that each semitone (in percentage terms) is equally spaced from its adjacent semitones.

The physics of some acoustic instruments is such that certain notes do not quite coincide with the correct tempered scale frequencies. In fact some electronic instruments have used methods of note generation that produced a similar result. Fortunately, the difference is usually small enough for most people to find it quite acceptable. These differences occur because some instruments do not enable all notes to be individually tuned (as in a piano) or controlled by the player (as with a violin). A fifth, for instance, is precisely 1.5 times higher in pitch than the root note with some instruments. This gives the fifth above middle A (at 440Hz) as 660Hz, whereas in the equal tempered scale it works out a fraction lower at 659.2418Hz. I suppose that the 660Hz figure has a mathematical perfection that is lacking in the equal tempered version. The problem with this mathematical precision is that notes have to shift slightly in frequency depending on which key you are playing in! The equal tempered scale gives what is a sort of averaged out scale that can accommodate any key. Most synthesizers and samplers are tuned to the well tempered scale, and this should all be of only academic importance.

The specification sheets for some instruments give the tuning range, and make reference to the minimum tuning increment as a certain number of 'cents'. In this sense, the word cent means one hundredth of a semitone. Some electronic instruments have continuous tuning, like a stringed instrument, and have what is theoretically infinite resolution. The accuracy of the tuning depends on how accurately you can adjust it. With modern digital electronic instruments the tuning is often variable in small jumps. In practice the increments are usually too small to be heard as such. There should certainly be no difficulty in tuning a digital instrument so accurately that any error is totally insignificant.

In the main you do not deal in frequencies when using synthesizers, but in terms of musical notes. It can still be useful to have some idea of what frequencies you are dealing with though, especially if you use sound samplers. Using these under certain circumstances gives a very restricted bandwidth that falls well short of the 20kHz notional upper limit of the audio range. Being aware of the frequencies you require the unit to handle can prevent you wasting your time trying the impossible.

Fig.1.2 shows the approximate frequency range covered by some acoustic instruments and the human voice. Note though, that these are the fundamental frequencies. As we shall see shortly, most sounds have a range of frequency components that stretch

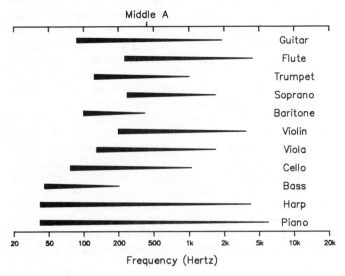

Figure 1.2 Frequency ranges for some common instruments

well beyond the fundamental frequency. It is difficult to give frequency ranges for electronic instruments as these vary substantially from one instrument to another. Most cover a fairly wide range, with five octaves being about the least one would expect these days. Some have a compass of around double this. It is not uncommon for electronic instruments to be restricted by their keyboards (which rarely go beyond 5 octaves) rather than by their electronics. It is quite normal to have an instrument with a compass of eight or nine octaves, but with a keyboard that only gives access to any five consecutive octaves in this range.

Waveforms

Something you are bound to encounter in equipment manuals, or even on the front panels of equipment, are waveform diagrams. These are really a form of graph, and they plot sound pressure on the vertical (Y) axis versus time on the horizontal (X) axis. Fig.1.3 shows a couple of example waveforms. In the upper waveform there are twice as many cycles in a given period of time, and it therefore has double the frequency of the lower waveform. In musical terms, it is the same note, but one octave higher.

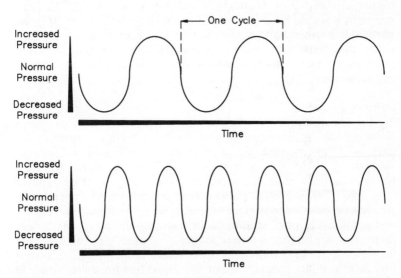

Figure 1.3 A waveform diagram is a graph showing air pressure versus time

All acoustic instruments have some form of resonator (or multiple resonators), such as the strings of a violin. If you were to attach a pen to the string of a violin, and then drag a piece of paper past the nib of the pen while bowing the string, the output waveform of the instrument would be drawn out on the paper. This is an over-simplification in that it assumes that the pen does not hinder the normal vibration of the string. More importantly, it also ignores the effect of the violin's body on the sound. Strictly speaking the waveform of an instrument can only be accurately determined by measuring the sound waves it produces. However, the sound produced is normally related closely to the physical vibrations of the resonator, and you might find it easier to visualize what waveforms are all about by looking at things in these purely mechanical terms.

Sinewaves
The waveforms shown in Fig.1.3 are known as sinewaves. The sinewave is an all-important waveform, as it could reasonably be regarded as the basic building block for sounds. Its important characteristic is that it contains just a single frequency. Any other waveform contains at least two frequencies, and for repetitive waveforms these are the fundamental frequency plus one or more harmonics. Harmonics are merely multiples of the fundamental frequency, and with a fundamental signal at (say) 100Hz, the harmonics would be at 200Hz, 300Hz, 400Hz, 500Hz, etc. It is the particular harmonics that are present and how strong (or other- wise) that they are, that accounts for the fact that different instruments sound totally unalike, even though they are playing the same note.

Other waveforms
Fig.1.4 shows some sample waveforms together with diagrams showing the relative strengths of the lower order harmonics for each one. This method of analyzing sounds is known as 'Fourier' analysis. You do not need to worry too much about the exact harmonics present in these basic waveforms, or their relative strengths. The important point is that smooth waveforms such as sinewaves, or even triangular waves, have a low harmonic content and a relatively pure sound. In fact a pure sinewave has a very distinctive sound that is unmistakable. The time 'pips' on the radio are sinewaves, as are the test tones many radio stations transmit just after the last programme of the night has finished. You will need a good quality radio (and preferably a good hi-fi system) if

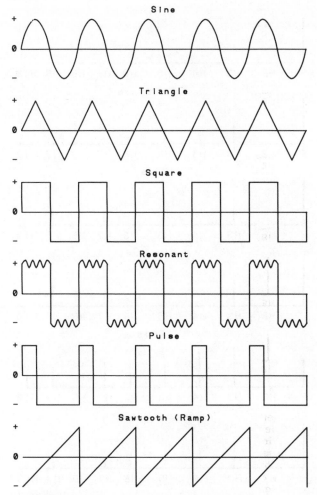

Figure 1.4 (a) Some common synthesizer waveforms

you want to hear these signals properly. The average transistor radio adds significant distortion which compromises the purity of the output sound and loses the characteristic sinewave sound.

The more spiky waveforms with their fast rising and (or) falling edges produce much stronger harmonics and a much harsher sound. A 'bright' sound is the more usual description. The resonant waveform is an interesting one, and one that can be

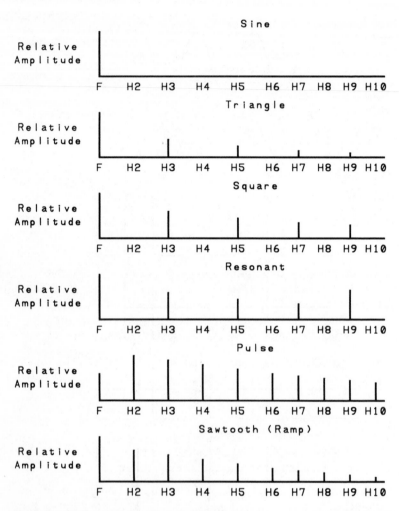

Figure 1.4 (b) The spectra for the waveforms of (a)

obtained by one method or another from most synthesizers. It consists mainly of the fundamental frequency plus one very strong harmonic. This is virtually two tones merged together, and the sound obtained depends very much on which harmonic is the emphasized one. Provided the harmonic is not a very high one, the sound is usually quite a rich and harmonious one.

You are likely to encounter references to 'second harmonics', 'third harmonics', etc. The convention is that the harmonic at double the fundamental frequency is the second harmonic, the one at three times the fundamental is the third harmonic, and so on. Logically one might consider the harmonic at double the fundamental to be the first harmonic rather than the second, but the universally accepted convention does not have things this way. With this convention the fundamental could be termed the first harmonic, but it never seems to be referred to as such.

Unharmonious sounds

Noise

Not all sounds have simple repetitive waveforms. Some contain frequencies that are not harmonically related, and these are mainly noise and metallic sounds. Noise signals are perhaps the easier to understand. These are random waveforms which follow no fixed pattern. In terms of their sound, they are 'hissing' type sounds. In terms of their frequency content, basic noise signals contain (in theory) all frequencies. The two standard forms of noise are the 'white' and 'pink' varieties. White noise contains all frequencies at equal strength, and is a fairly high pitched hissing sound. The background noise on radio reception, cassette tapes during playback, etc. is (more or less) white noise. Pink noise has the frequencies in octave bands at equal strength. In other words, the signal strength from 100Hz to 200Hz is the same as from 200Hz to 400Hz. With white noise there would be equal strength in the signal from 100Hz to 200Hz and 200Hz to 300Hz. Pink noise therefore has less high frequency content, and is lower pitched. It is often likened to gently falling rain, and is a rather more soothing sound than the relatively energetic white noise.

Metallic sounds

Metallic sounds such as gongs and bells differ from most other instruments in that they are generated by two or three dimensional resonators. The strings of a violin, tubes of brass instruments, etc., are essentially one dimensional. The longer the effective lengths of these resonators, the lower their pitch. The more strongly they are vibrated, the greater the harmonic content in their sounds. This gives them comparatively simple sounds, and sounds that are relatively easy to synthesize. With two and three dimensional resonators such as gongs and bells there are effectively a number of fundamental signals, plus harmonics of these signals. These can

9

interact to produce a very complex sound that is less easy to synthesize. As we shall see later though, it can be done.

Although metallic sounds contain non-harmonically related frequencies, they are not necessarily non-musically related frequencies. In fact most instruments of this type produce tones that are musically related (often fifths apart) so that a rich and harmonious sound is obtained. They can produce decidedly discordant results if the fundamental tones do not have suitable musical relationships.

Sound advice

These basic types of sound give great variety, but do not account for the enormous range of sounds that can be produced. There are two other important factors that greatly affect the way things sound, and massively increase the range of sounds that can be generated. These both relate to how sounds change from their beginning to their end.

Envelope

The most fundamental way in which a sound varies during its course is the variation in its volume. This can have a much more drastic effect on the nature of a sound than you might think. The way in which a signal varies in volume is called its envelope, and this is normally represented as a simple graph of volume (vertical axis) versus time (horizontal axis). Fig.1.5 shows the envelope

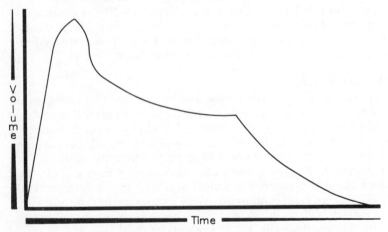

Figure 1.5 A piano type envelope shape

shape for piano type sounds. Here there is an almost instant rise to full volume initially, followed by a quite fast fall in volume. The sound then reaches a plateau where there is a very slow drop in volume, followed by a relatively fast decay period (once the key of the piano has been released).

In the envelope shape of Fig.1.6 there is again a fast attack, but then the sound decays quite quickly and continues to do so until it has dropped to a very low volume. A harp string being plucked is a good example of this form of envelope. A lot of instruments have a simple envelope shape of the type shown in Fig.1.7 where

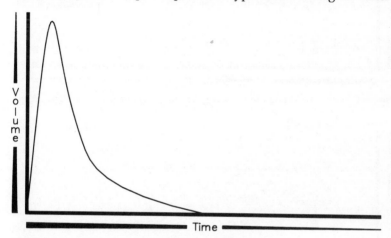

Figure 1.6 The plucked instrument envelope shape

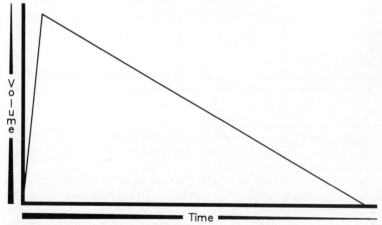

Figure 1.7 The envelope shape for guitars and many other instruments

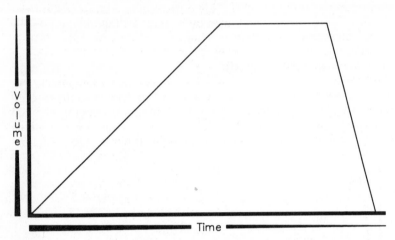

Figure 1.8 The slow attack and fast decay of this envelope gives a strange effect

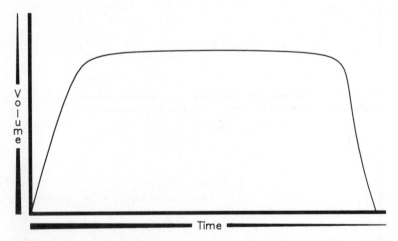

Figure 1.9 The envelope shape for many string and wind instruments

the sound rises almost instantly to full volume and then dies away gradually over a period of time. Most guitars have an envelope shape not far removed from this.

The envelope shape of Fig.1.8 is one that gives an unusual sound. It is more or less the inverse of the previous envelope shape, with a long and steady build up in volume followed by a very rapid cut off at the end. If you process the output from an electric guitar to give it this kind of envelope shape, the resultant sound is very weird indeed. In fact it sounds more like an out-of-sorts organ than a guitar! I suppose the reason that this type of envelope sounds strange is that it is not the natural envelope of any acoustic instrument (or none that I know of anyway). Obviously with some acoustic instruments (such as wind and string instruments) the envelope is largely controlled by the player. However, with these instruments the envelope shape is normally something along the lines of Fig.1.9. The instruments could be played to produce an envelope shape similar to Fig.1.8, but probably only with some difficulty, and this type of envelope seems to be virtually unheard of in the world of acoustic instruments. It can be achieved quite easily with electronic instruments though, and is sometimes used to good effect.

All change

The changes in a sound over the period of its envelope are not necessarily uniform changes in all its component frequencies. Few (if any) natural sounds have the same frequency content from beginning to end, and in most cases there are drastic changes during the course of a signal. If you view the output waveform from a guitar using a device called an oscilloscope, you could be forgiven for thinking that you were viewing the waveforms from three or four instruments rather than the changes in the output from a single instrument!

With many acoustic instruments the sound starts out at quite high volume, and the strong vibration of the resonator gives a sound output that is rich in strong harmonics. As the volume dies away and the resonator vibrates less strongly, it gives a much more rounded output waveform that has a relatively weak harmonic content. In other words, each harmonic has a separate envelope shape which does not necessarily mimic the overall envelope shape of the signal. Some sounds are quite complex, and a certain harmonic (or harmonics) might actually increase in amplitude at some point in the envelope before decaying away to nothing. There are various ways of depicting the way in which the harmonic content of a signal changes over a period of time, but the 'mountain range' graph is probably the most common. An example graph of this type is shown in Fig.1.10. This is really just separate envelope diagrams for each frequency component in the signal,

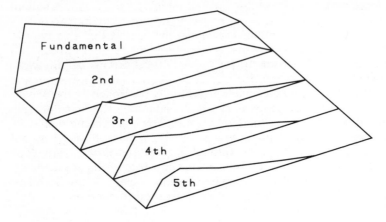

Figure 1.10 A 3-D style display is sometimes used to show separate envelopes for the fundamental and harmonics

with a 3-D style view so that the separate elements of the graph stand out quite well from one another.

Recapitulation

If we summarize the important characteristics that distinguish one sound from another, they are as follows:

1 Pitch
Some people are literally tone deaf, and cannot tell one note from another even if they have well separated pitches. Those of a musical bent normally have a very good sense of pitch, and for them this is perhaps the most obvious difference between two totally different sounds.

2 Harmonics
Two signals can have the same pitch but still sound totally different. One reason for this is that most sounds contain more than one frequency. These frequencies are normally the fundamental plus multiples of this frequency which are called harmonics. Some sounds (particularly metallic sounds) contain non-harmonically related frequencies, or random (noise) frequencies, giving further ranges of sounds.

3 Envelope

The way the volume of a sound changes from its beginning to its end has more effect on the way it sounds than most people would expect. Changes in the harmonic content during the course of a sound provide further variations, and what are not necessarily subtle differences between sounds.

Making waves

Making sound waves of various types using acoustic instruments is simple enough, and is accomplished using different types of resonator, plus a variety of methods for vibrating them. How are sounds generated electronically? The electronics do not actually generate any sounds whatever, but generate electric voltages that vary with time in much the same way that air pressure varies with time in sound waves. In an analogue synthesizer the processes involved could be regarded as analogous to acoustic sound generation, but with modern digital instruments the processes involved are quite different. In either case the output is still in the form of a varying voltage, having peaks of positive and negative voltage instead of the increased and reduced pressure of sound-waves. The varying voltages are generated by circuits called oscillators, and these circuits can be designed to provide a wide variety of output waveforms. This gives a useful range of sounds, but some processing of the basic signals is needed to give acceptable results. This is the subject of the next chapter.

The conversion from electrical signal to soundwave is made by the loudspeaker or headphones. These are mostly of the moving coil variety, and use a setup of the type outlined in Fig.1.11. The coil forms an electromagnet, and if a voltage is applied to it the coil has the normal magnetic poles. The polarity of the electromagnet depends on the polarity of the electric signal applied to the coil. With one polarity the fixed and electromagnets will have the same polarity, and unlike poles will be next to each other. The coil will then be attracted towards the fixed magnet, and will pull the diaphragm with it. If the signal applied to the coil is of the opposite polarity, like poles will be next to each other, and the coil will be repelled by the fixed magnet. It then moves forwards, again moving the diaphragm as it does so. The strength of the electromagnet, and the displacement of the coil and diaphragm, depends on the voltage applied to the coil. In an ideal loudspeaker there is a perfectly linear relationship between applied voltage and displacement of the diaphragm.

If we amplify the output of our synthesizer and apply the

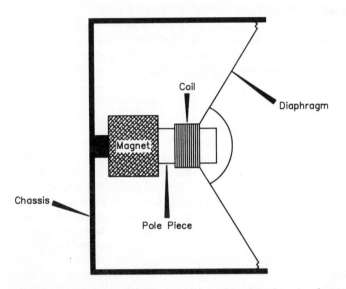

Figure 1.11 The system used in a moving coil loudspeaker. An electronic instrument must have some form of loudspeaker or headphone in order to produce sounds

boosted signal to the loudspeaker, the varying voltages produced by the instrument are converted into corresponding movements of the diaphragm. These in turn produce soundwaves, and what we hear sounds just like the instrument we are synthesizing.

Even though the physical properties of the loudspeaker may be nothing like the instrument we are trying to synthesize, with an accurate signal from the synthesizer and a good quality loudspeaker an amazingly accurate representation of the real thing can be obtained. On the other hand, with a poorly executed synthesis and (or) an inadequate audio system, results will probably be abysmal. Really good synthesis is much harder to achieve than mediocre results, but with modern equipment it is possible to produce some truly astounding results. With some additional electronics you can even add effects such as reverberation to give the synthesized signal a very realistic 'big hall' sound. Distinguishing between a synthesized sound and the real thing can be very difficult these days. Do not overlook the fact that synthesis is not wholly about imitating acoustic instruments. There are tremendous opportunities to produce sounds that are beyond the capabilities of acoustic instruments.

2 Analogue synthesis

At one time analogue synthesizers were the only synthesizers in common usage. Today there are few new instruments available which are truly analogue synthesizers. Despite this, we'll look at conventional analogue synthesis in some depth in this chapter. Analogue techniques have to a large extent been replaced with more modern digital circuits, but the old analogue system is a nice and easy-to-understand method of sound synthesis, and represents a good starting point for beginners. Analogue synthesis might be largely obsolete, but the principles involved are not. A point that should be kept in mind is that there are a lot of digital instruments which have analogue style controls. The labels above the controls are different in some cases, but their effect on sounds is very much the same as their conventional analogue counterparts. If you know how to control a conventional synthesizer, adapting to most (but not all) modern instruments poses no real problem.

Probably the main reason for the demise of analogue synthesizers was that they could not easily be controlled by a computer or other forms of digital control circuit. This is an important factor with today's complex polyphonic, multi-timbral instruments, whose flexibility invariably centres on a powerful microprocessor based control circuit. Their tendency to drift out of tune was almost certainly a contributory factor as well. Their sounds were and are very good though, and still preferred by many to today's digital wonders. For what it's worth, in my opinion modern instruments are much superior in the range and quality of sounds they offer. On the other hand, if analogue techniques had received the same amount of research and development as digital techniques, who knows what sounds analogue instruments would be producing by now?

Producing the sounds

In the 1970s, electronic keyboards really started to become popular, and the basic choice was between an organ or a synthesizer.

Usually the first question asked by prospective electronic music makers was 'what is the difference between the two types of instrument?' At that time the differences were massive, with the most obvious one being that organs offered what was in many cases polyphony that was only limited by the number of keys on the keyboard. Synthesizers, by contrast, usually only provided monophonic output (i.e. you could play only one note at a time)!

The real difference between the two instruments lay in the basic way in which they generated their output signals. A 'real' organ has pipes to generate the notes, with a pipe of a different length for each note. Electronic organs usually mimicked this by having a separate oscillator for each note. Each oscillator was electronically tuned to accurately generate a signal at the right frequency for its particular note. When you pressed a key you switched on the corresponding oscillator, and the appropriate note was generated. With a separate sound generator for each note you could have as many notes playing simultaneously as you required. The limiting factor was the number of keys you could operate rather than any technical limitations of the instrument.

The problem with this arrangement was that it required an extravagant amount of electronics with some 61 oscillators being needed in order to give the typical coverage of five octaves. Also, there was limited scope for providing a really varied range of sounds. If you wanted five different output waveforms, then each oscillator had to be switchable to these five waveforms. Processing the outputs of the oscillators is a much more simple way of altering the sound, but this method only permits relatively limited variations in the sounds produced unless each output signal is processed separately. Separate processing is impracticable as it requires such a large number of processing circuits.

Voltage controlled oscillator

The analogue synthesizer was a totally different concept. It was designed first and foremost as a means of producing a varied range of sounds. Polyphony was very much a secondary consideration, and except on some very expensive instruments it was absent. The basis of an analogue synthesizer is the VCO (voltage controlled oscillator). The pitch of the VCO is controlled by an input voltage, and the source of this voltage is the keyboard circuit. The higher the input voltage, the higher the pitch of the output. In practice the system must be accurately set up so that the keyboard provides a series of voltages that give a chromatic scale from the VCO.

Lin or log

Most early synthesizers had a linear control characteristic, which means that there is a linear relationship between the control voltage and the output frequency. If an input of 1 volt gives an output of 100Hz, then inputs of 2 volts, 3 volts, 4 volts, etc. will respectively produce pitches of 200Hz, 300Hz, 400Hz, etc. This is the natural control characteristic of the VCOs used in these synthesizers.

Virtually all the later analogue synthesizers utilized what became a standard logarithmic characteristic of 1 volt per octave. In other words, if a control voltage of 1 volt produces an output frequency of 110Hz, then input voltages of 2 volts, 3 volts, and 4 volts would give respective output frequencies of 220Hz, 440Hz, and 880 Hz. This is not the natural control characteristic of a VCO, and it is achieved by adding a non-linear amplifier ahead of the VCO. This distorts the input voltage to match it to the linear characteristic of the VCO.

The addition of this non-linear amplifier complicated the electronics. The tuning drift for which analogue synthesizers are infamous is almost always due to drift in this amplifier rather than drift in the oscillator itself. Outweighing these drawbacks are the convenience with which the keyboard voltages can be generated. Fig.2.1 shows example voltages for a range of notes, and the salient point here is that the increment from one note to the next is always the same. This is 83.33 millivolts (0.08333 volts), which is what you get if you divide the 1 volt per octave step by the twelve semitones in each octave. This can be generated very easily in the keyboard

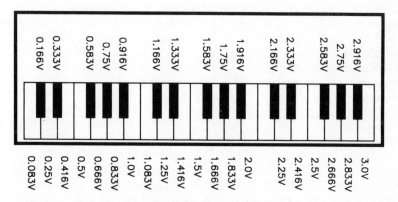

Figure 2.1 Keyboard voltages for a 'log' synthesizer

circuit, with a minimal amount of setting up being required. It was also very convenient for the later analogue synthesizers which were computer controlled, and used digital circuits to produce the keyboard circuits. Standard converter circuits can be used to produce the appropriate voltages from the digital values provided by the microprocessor control circuit.

The problem with the linear control characteristic is that it has a voltage increment from one semitone to the next that depends on the two notes concerned. The higher up the musical scale, the greater the voltage step from one note to the next. This point is demonstrated by Fig.2.2 which is the linear equivalent of Fig.2.1.

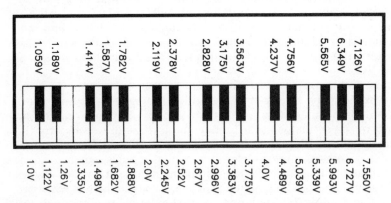

Figure 2.2 Example linear control keyboard voltages. The increment from one note to the next is not a constant amount

In order to obtain a suitable progression of voltages, either custom made precision components are required, or a lot of very careful setting up of adjustable components must be undertaken. Most synthesizers have control voltage inputs and outputs so that one instrument can control another. This will only work properly with two linear synthesizers or two logarithmic types, not one of each type.

Shaping the envelope generator

A keyboard plus a VCO does not really constitute a viable musical instrument. The VCO is switched on all the time, and simply follows the pitch dictated by the keyboard circuit. With no key pressed the output frequency would be indeterminate as there

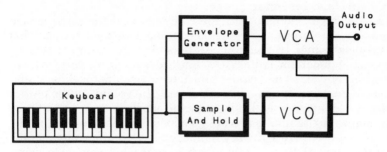

Figure 2.3 The minimal synthesizer block diagram

would then be no output voltage from the keyboard circuit. There is no envelope shaping of the output signal, and each note would carry straight on from the previous one with no proper beginning or end to a piece of music played on the device!. A minimal synthesizer would use the arrangement depicted in Fig.2.3.

Problems with the pitch wandering are solved by the sample and hold circuit. This simply 'remembers' the last voltage supplied by the keyboard, and maintains this as the input potential to the VCO when no key of the keyboard is being pressed. Some sample and hold circuits work better than others, but most will accurately hold a note for at least a few seconds after a key has been released. This is adequate in practice.

Envelope shaping is handled by the envelope generator and the VCA (voltage controlled amplifier). This aspect of synthesizers tends to cause a certain amount of confusion as many people seem to get the idea that a VCA is an envelope shaper, while others think that the envelope generator provides this function. In fact the two of them in unison constitute an envelope shaper, which varies the volume of the output signal to give the desired effect. The VCA is the device which actually handles the output signal from the VCO, and provides the variations in volume. Like a VCO, the VCA is controlled by an input voltage, and the envelope shaper provides a varying output voltage that gives the required changes in volume. Incidentally, just about anything in a synthesizer that can be voltage controlled normally is. This offers tremendous versatility with signals from one part of the unit being routed through to control other parts of the instrument. It is primarily this factor that distinguishes synthesizers from other electronic musical instruments.

21

AD envelope generator

The envelope generator is triggered by the keyboard, and it then provides an output signal that is controlled by the user via what is usually either two or four controls. The most simple type of envelope generator is the AD (attack, decay) type. This has two controls which, as one would probably expect, are the 'attack' and 'decay' controls. When a key is pressed, the volume of the output signal rises at a rate which is set by the attack control. The volume continues to rise until it reaches its maximum possible level, or the key is released. Once the key has been released, the volume of the output signal falls at a rate which is controlled using the decay control.

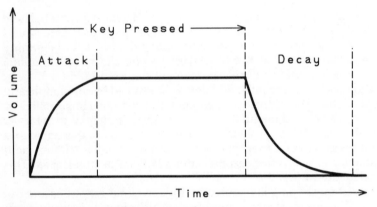

Figure 2.4 The basics of A/D envelope shaping

Fig.2.4 should help you to visualize the way in which this type of envelope shaping operates. It can produce some quite good sounds, but it does not really cater for all types of sound. In particular, it is no use for sounds that have a high initial volume followed by a much lower sustained level. With an AD envelope generator the sustained level is always maximum volume.

ADSR envelope generator

Most synthesizers are equipped with a more sophisticated envelope shaper of the ADSR (attack, decay, sustain, release) type. This has four controls, one for each phase of the envelope's characteristic. Fig.2.5 illustrates the way in which this type of envelope shaper controls the sound.

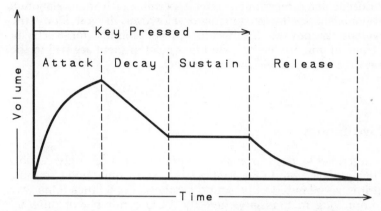

Figure 2.5 An ADSR shaper permits more complex shapes to be produced

The attack phase is much the same as the attack part of the AD envelope shape. It controls the rate at which the volume rises to its peak level. However, once this peak level has been reached, the sound starts to drop in volume even if the key is not released. This is the decay section of the envelope, and the decay control is used to set the rate at which the signal drops in volume. When the volume reaches a certain level it remains at this level, and does not start to fall until the key is released. This is the sustain phase of the envelope, and the sustain control sets the signal level at which the decay part of the envelope finishes. It differs from the other envelope shaper controls which set rates of rise or fall, not signal levels. Once the key is released the signal dies away to zero at a rate set using the release control.

Of course, if a new note is struck almost immediately, the release phase ends at once and the attack phase of the next note is commenced. This is the same as an acoustic instrument where one note does not wait for the previous one to die away to zero before it starts! If the key is released before the sustain period is reached, then the release period is begun as soon as the key is released and the sustain period is omitted. In fact the decay period will be omitted if the key is released early enough, and the attack period may also be cut short.

An ADSR envelope shaper is reasonably simple, and is quite straightforward to use. It enables the envelopes of many acoustic instruments to be quite accurately copied, as well as permitting weird and wonderful envelopes with no natural counterparts to be produced. Some recent instruments permit much more elaborate envelope shapes to be generated. However, if you study the envelope shapes of the factory preset sounds for such an instrument you are likely to find that most of them are within the repertoire of an ADSR envelope shaper.

Wave options

As described so far, our analogue synthesizer is certainly capable of being played, and may well produce some quite good sounds, but it is very limited in its sound synthesis capabilities. One way of improving matters is to give the VCO a number of different output waveforms. This is indeed a standard feature for synthesizers, but the exact waveforms provided vary from one instrument to another. Popular waveforms are triangle, variable pulse, and sawtooth. A few provide a sinewave option, but this is relatively rare, and is not necessarily a particularly useful waveform. As we shall see later, it is quite easy to obtain a reasonable sinewave signal from the triangular waveform.

Pulse width control
The variable pulse signal is a useful one. A front panel 'pulse width' control usually enables the waveform to be varied from a narrow positive pulse, through to a squarewave, and on through to a narrow negative pulse (Fig.2.6). In fact a narrow positive pulse does not sound any different from a negative one of the same width. There is a large difference between the squarewave and pulse signals though. A squarewave has a strong harmonic content, and gives a very bright sound. It also has a strong fundamental signal. The narrow pulse signal also has a strong harmonic content, but the fundamental signal is relatively weak. The narrower the pulse width is made, the weaker the fundamental signal becomes. This produces a very thin and buzzy sound.

The triangular waveform is an important one as it has a relatively weak harmonic content. It is therefore well suited to synthesizing the sounds of instruments with dull sounds. A sinewave signal is simply too pure for most purposes, and is absent from most synthesizers. A useful feature is the ability to select more than one waveform, so that two or more waveforms can be mixed in order to produce more elaborate shapes.

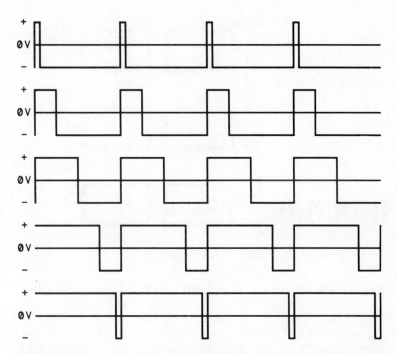

Figure 2.6 The pulse width control permits the waveform to be adjusted from a narrow positive pulse through to a narrow negative one

Filtering

Having various wave shapes available greatly expands the range of sounds available from the synthesizer, but it still leaves it very limited in one extremely important respect. The waveform of most acoustic instruments varies quite considerably from the beginning of the sound to its end. Without these changes in wave shape sounds tend to be rather uninteresting and lifeless. Our improved minimal synthesizer has no means of introducing these changes in wave shape, and is likely to give sounds that might seem to be quite good initially, but would probably soon become boring and uninspiring.

The improved version (Fig.2.7) overcomes this problem by adding a filter at the output. This setup lacks frills, but represents a perfectly usable instrument that will provide a very useful range

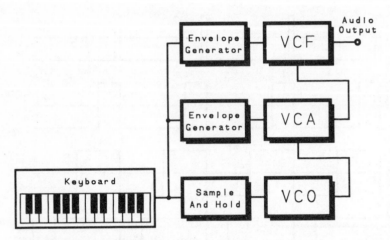

Figure 2.7 The improved synthesizer block diagram

of sounds. The filter at the output needs to be a fairly sophisticated affair though, and would normally be something far more advanced than the tone controls of a hi-fi amplifier. Fixed filters of this type do not really fit the current requirements. By altering the relative strengths of the fundamental and harmonic components of the signal they would certainly alter the wave shape. However, the waveform would still remain the same throughout the duration of the signal, as the filtering would remain constant.

Voltage controlled filter
What we require is a filter that can alter its characteristics during the course of the signal. This is achieved by using a VCF (voltage controlled filter) controlled from an envelope generator which is in turn controlled from the keyboard. The filter would usually be of the lowpass type. This means that it passes signals up to certain frequencies, and then above that frequency it provides progressive attenuation. In other words, the higher the frequency of a signal is above the 'cutoff' frequency, the more it is reduced by the filter.

Some synthesizers have other types of filtering available, and the three other possible types are highpass, bandpass and notch filtering. Highpass is simply the opposite of lowpass filtering, with signals above a certain threshold frequency being passed normally. Below that cutoff frequency signals are progressively attenuated. Whereas lowpass filtering permits the fundamental signal to pass

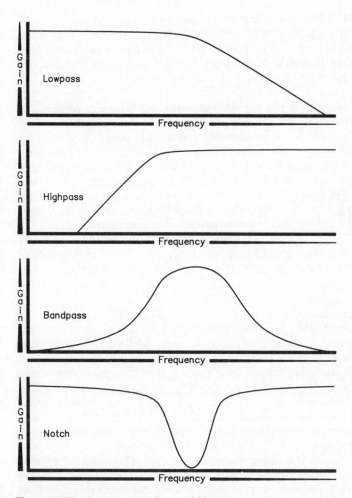

Figure 2.8 The four standard forms of filtering

but attenuates some or all of the harmonics, highpass filtering passes some or all of the harmonics but attenuates the fundamental (and possibly some of the lower harmonics). Lowpass filtering mellows a bright sound, whereas highpass filtering gives a thin and buzzy sound.

Bandpass filtering is a sort of combined highpass/lowpass filtering. Signals over a narrow range of frequencies are passed normally, but above or below this band there is strong attenuation.

The effect of bandpass filtering is very much dependent on where the centre frequency is placed relative to the fundamental input frequency. It also depends on how wide the passband is made. In many cases it would not sound much different to highpass or lowpass filtering. This type of filtering is not available on many synthesizers.

Notch filtering is the opposite of bandpass filtering, and signals at most frequencies pass straight through to the output. It is only over a narrow band of frequencies that signals are attenuated. This type of filtering is the least obvious, and with a fixed operating frequency it may not affect the sound at all. With a complex input signal that contains a broad range of frequencies the result is a subtle effect that gives a sort of strange hollow sound. With the filter frequency varied the effect is more obvious, and a sort of very basic phaser type effect is obtained.

Fig.2.8 gives a graphical representation of all four types of filtering and this should help to clarify the differences between them.

Attenuation rates
In the specifications for equipment that includes filters you will normally encounter references to so many decibels (dB). Although decibels are generally thought of as a measurement of the loudness of sounds, they are actually used as a general purpose logarithmic measurement. The gain of an amplifier could simply be specified as a certain number of times. If an input of 0.1 volts gives an output at 1 volt, then the gain is obviously equal to ten times (1/0.1 = 10). This is using simple linear measurement, which is adequate for many purposes.

In electronics it is often necessary to deal in very large figures, and a logarithmic scale is then often more convenient. On the decibel scale a voltage gain of ten times is a gain of 20dB. A further gain of ten times would be an overall gain of one hundred times, but in decibel terms would be 40dB (i.e. 20dB + 20dB = 40dB and not 20dB × 20dB = 400dB). If a signal passes through a number of stages, it is just a matter of adding up the gains of these stages in decibels to arrive at the overall gain figure. Losses are easily handled by this system, and are expressed as negative amounts (e.g. −20dB means signals will be reduced by a factor of ten).

Strictly speaking this is not a valid way of using decibels, which are really intended for power gain and not voltage gain (which does not take into account the amount of current flowing in the input and output circuits). In practice decibels are a very convenient way of handling voltage gain, and are probably used more in this way than for power gain measurements.

When applied to filters you will usually encounter decibels in the form of 'x' number of decibels per octave. This is a measure of how rapidly the filtering is applied. For a lowpass filter a figure of 6dB per octave means that doubling the frequency of the signal causes the gain of the filter to reduce by half. For a highpass type a halving of frequency causes a 50% reduction in voltage gain. Actually a reduction in gain by 50% is not a loss of precisely 6dB, but the error is so small that it is almost invariably ignored. Filter attenuation rates are normally in multiples of 6dB per octave, and most synthesizers have 24dB per octave filters. This means that (for a lowpass filter) each doubling of frequency results in the gain of the filter dropping by a factor of 16. Of course, this only applies on the part of the filter's response where it is applying the filtering—not in the passband.

Fig.2.9 shows the idealized responses for lowpass filters having attenuation rates of 6, 12, 24 and 36dB per octave. Although modern filters have very high levels of performance, none of them truly achieves this ideal level of performance. There is never an instant transition from zero filtering to the full attenuation rate. There is always a more gentle roll-off before the full attenuation rate is achieved.

There seems to be a popular misconception in electronic music circles that the higher the attenutation rate of the filters the better the synthesizer will perform. This is quite definitely not the case.

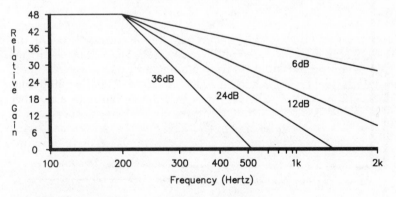

Figure 2.9 Lowpass filtering with different attenuation rates

A low attenuation rate will not give good results because the effect of the filtering will be inadequate to have a really marked effect on sounds. A very high attenuation rate will give some interesting effects, but is a bit obvious in operation and unsuitable for general use. Ideally it would be possible to vary the attenuation rate, or to at least have several switch selectable rates. These seem to be rare features though, and most instruments have a single roll-off rate. If only a single attenutation rate is available, then 24dB per octave probably represents the best compromise.

Resonance

Most VCFs have a resonance control, and without one of these it is impossible to obtain some of the most interesting sounds. With the resonance control set at minimum the filter operates normally. As this control is advanced, a peak is produced in the frequency response of the filter at or very near the cutoff frequency. Advancing the control produces an increasingly pronounced peak in the response (Fig.2.10). With a lot of VCFs you have to be careful not to over-do the resonance, as they can break into oscillation and act as another VCO (something that can sometimes be put to good use).

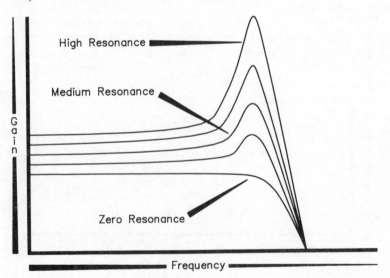

Figure 2.10 The effect of advancing the resonance control

With moderate resonance and a fixed filter frequency the result is rather nasal sounds. Usually the filter frequency would be varied during the course of a sound, and this would give a slightly richer and more lively sound. Strong resonance and sweeping of the filter gives a very distinctive type of sound. A guitarist's waa-waa pedal effect is produced using a lowpass filter with fairly strong resonance.

When using filters, or any part of a synthesizer for that matter, it is best to think directly in terms of the sounds produced by different control settings. However, initially you might find it helpful to visualize the frequency components in the input signal imposed on the frequency response graph of the filter (Fig.2.11).

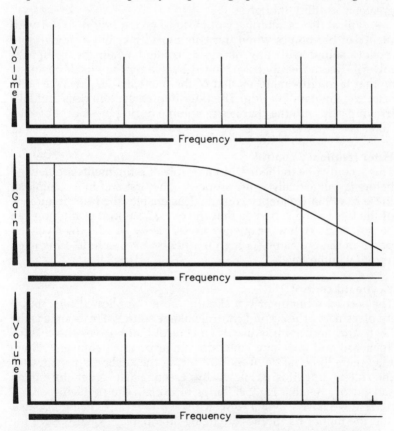

Figure 2.11 Superimposing the components of a signal on a frequency response graph makes it easy to visualize the effect of the filtering

It is then quite easy to visualize the effect of the filtering, and to mentally convert this into the sound that will result from it.

In control

The control voltage for the filter is derived from two sources, although you only need to use one or other of these. The main source is an envelope generator, which would normally be an exact copy of the one which drives the VCA. In a low cost instrument the same envelope generator could in fact be used for both the VCA and the VCF. Separate envelope generators afford much greater versatility though.

A typical use of filtering would be to give a bright sound with plenty of harmonics when the volume is high, but a much more mellow sound with low harmonic content when the volume is lower. This can easily be achieved by setting the envelope shape so that it roughly matches that of the one used for the VCA, and selecting lowpass filtering. The filter frequency then rises and falls in sympathy with the changes in volume during the course of each note.

Filter frequency control
This sounds fine in theory, but a couple of refinements are needed before it will actually work properly. The first and most simple of these is a filter frequency control. This enables the basic frequency of the filter to be varied so that the overall amount of filtering can be adjusted. A low frequency gives plenty of filtering even on peaks in the envelope—a high frequency gives little filtering even at low volume levels.

Keyboard control
The second refinement is a slightly more complicated one, and it involves using the second control voltage source. This source is the keyboard, and there is usually a control that enables the relative keyboard and envelope generator amounts to be adjusted. There may seem to be no point in introducing the keyboard voltage into the filter, but this is normally essential in order to obtain satisfactory results. Fig.2.12 helps to explain the problem.

Here we have a signal to which some filtering is being applied, and the higher harmonics are being attenuated. We also have the same signal but an octave higher (represented by the broken lines). With this signal the harmonics are much more severely filtered,

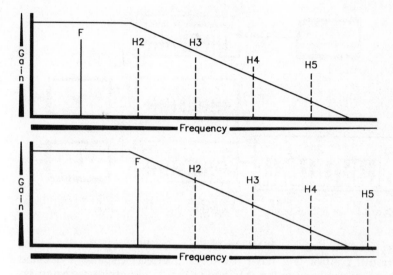

Figure 2.12 A fixed VCF frequency effectively gives different filtering on each note

and there would be a marked change in the sound. The filter frequency remaining the same and the note being raised by an octave is much the same as the note remaining the same and filter frequency being reduced by an octave. The filter frequency is effectively different for each note. For very low pitched notes there would be very little filtering, while very high pitched notes could be affected to such an extent that even the fundamental signal would be severely attenuated.

The VCF has the same control characteristic as the VCO, and by feeding the keyboard voltage through to the VCF it can be made to precisely track the VCO so that consistent results are obtained over the full range of the keyboard. Play a note an octave higher than the previous note, and the VCF will operate an octave higher than on the previous note. Most synthesizers are much more versatile than this, and have an arrangement of the type outlined in Fig.2.13. Here the voltages from the keyboard, envelope generator, and frequency control are combined in a mixer before being applied to the VCF. This mixer gives control over the relative strengths of the keyboard and envelope generator voltages. If you want the filter frequency to precisely match the VCO's frequency, then some careful adjustment of the controls will provide this. If, on the other hand, you would prefer the filter to provide slightly

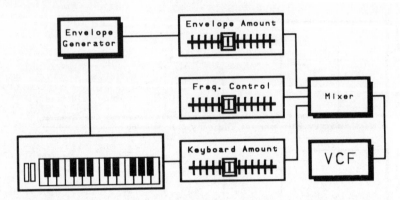

Figure 2.13 The VCF is normally controlled by three signal sources

stronger filtering on high notes, then backing off the keyboard amount control will have the desired effect. Usually a boosted keyboard amount can be obtained so that higher notes are brighter. The more options you have the greater the range of sounds the instrument can produce.

Hearing double

This basic arrangement of synthesizer building blocks provides quite a powerful instrument, and one that is capable of a massive range of useful sounds. Most synthesizers offer a number of additional features though, and can provide an even greater range of sounds. It is not possible to give details of all these frills here, but we will consider the main ones as well as some of the more rare features.

Second VCO

Probably the most useful extra feature is a second VCO. This could have its own signal processing stages, but it would normally have its output mixed with the signal from the first VCO. This might not seem to offer much scope for improved sounds, but it is surprising what a difference it can make. If you go through the factory preset sounds for a synthesizer which has the capability of using two VCOs, you will probably be hard pressed to find one that utilizes only a single oscillator.

With the two VCOs set to precisely the same frequency the

second VCO has no effect. In practice the two VCOs would normally be set with one at a fractionally different frequency to the other (it would probably be impossible to get them precisely in step anyway). This can give a very basic chorus type effect, so that it sounds like two instruments playing in unison, and it certainly give a much richer sound. If you play a two VCO sound and then switch to the single VCO equivalent it is surprising how flat the single VCO version usually sounds. Incidentally, there are plenty of acoustic instruments which have two resonators and which require a two VCO synthesizer in order to accurately mimic them (including some string and woodwind instruments).

Phased out

In terms of the output waveform, the effect is as shown in Fig.2.14. In order to understand what is happening here you must understand the important subject of signal phasing. Phase is measured in degrees, and there are 360 degrees in one cycle. If you study a few waveforms you will see that the line goes through 180 degrees on the first half cycle, and then 180 degrees in the opposite direction on the next half cycle, giving 360 degrees per cycle. If one signal lags another by half a cycle, they would be said to be 180

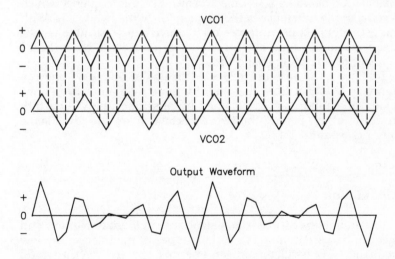

Figure 2.14 The lower waveform is the result of mixing the upper two waveforms

degrees out of phase. A phase lag of 90 degrees means that one signal lags another by one quarter of a cycle.

Simple mixing of two signals produces an output signal that at any instant in time is equal to the sum of the two input voltages. Remember that the voltage is positive on the top set of half cycles, and negative on the bottom set. Two positive signals add together to give a stronger positive output. Similarly, two negative signals add together to give a stronger negative output. One positive going and one negative going signal produce a cancelling effect, and a weaker output signal. With the two signals at slightly different frequencies they continuously move in and out of phase, giving the effect shown in Fig.2.14. The lower waveform was derived by sampling the two VCO waveforms at regular intervals, and using the sum of their amplitudes to give a series of plot points. Much more frequent sampling would be needed in order to produce a really accurate prediction of the output waveform. However, this diagram is accurate enough to show the overall effect.

This effect is for the signals to add together when they are in-phase, so that a strong output signal is obtained. As they go out of phase there is a cancelling effect. This tends to flatten the output waveform and give a low output voltage. At some points the two signals are equal but opposite, and zero output is obtained. The output signal therefore rises and falls in amplitude continuously. This can be heard as a so-called 'beat-note' at a frequency which is equal to the difference in the frequencies of the two VCOs. With the oscillators almost at the same frequency the beat note is well in the sub-audio range, and is not audible as a note. It can be heard as a sort of throbbing sound though.

The two VCOs are not restricted to use in this way, one can normally be offset from the other by more than an octave. Some good 'fat' sounds can be obtained by offsetting one VCO a fifth from the other. Setting the two an octave apart also gives some very rich sounds.

Modulation

A low frequency oscillator is a standard synthesizer feature, and this can be used to provide various types of modulation. By low frequency (LF) oscillator I mean one that operates over a typical frequency range of 0.1Hz to 10Hz. Its fundamental signal, and probably many of the harmonics, are therefore below the lower limit of the audio spectrum and are consequently inaudible. Although the signal from the low frequency oscillator is inaudible, it can introduce effects that are very audible. The low frequency oscillator may offer a variety of wave shapes, but for most purposes only waveforms that have a low harmonic content work well. Triangular and sinewave outputs are the ones that are best for most types of modulation.

Vibrato
The most basic form of modulation is frequency modulation. This is obtained by using the output of the oscillator to modulate (vary) the keyboard voltage slightly. Instead of each note being at a fixed frequency, it then varies slightly either side of this frequency at a rate which is controlled by the low frequency oscillator. This is the standard 'vibrato' effect, and is one that can be obtained from a number of acoustic instruments (fretless string instruments for example, or a guitar which has a vibrato attachment). You can get some good phasing effects with a twin VCO synthesizer by modulating one VCO but not the other.

You will find pitch and modulation wheels on most synthesizers. These are large rotary (edge-type) controls, and the modulation wheel permits quick and easy adjustment of the modulation level. The maximum depth of frequency modulation is generally quite limited, but a strongly frequency modulated output tends to provide interesting sounds that are of limited musical value. I suppose the problem is that to the human ear a signal of this type tends to be of indeterminate pitch. Not much use for the lead line! The pitch wheel enables the pitch of the instrument to be varied either side of its normal level so that manual vibrato can be provided.

Tremolo
The other standard form of modulation is the amplitude type. This uses the low frequency oscillator to vary the volume of the output signal (Fig. 2.15), and gives the 'tremolo' effect. This is a milder effect than vibrato unless very strong modulation is used. Although very popular at one time this form of modulation is not used a great deal these days. It is very useful for enlivening the sounds of single VCO synthesizers.

Although the effect of tremolo on the output signal may seem very similar to having two VCOs at slightly different frequencies, it is not the same. With two VCOs there is a complex output signal

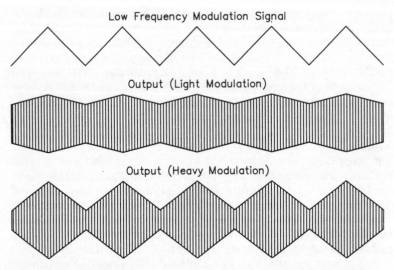

Figure 2.15 Tremolo is produced by using the LFO to amplitude modulate the output from the VCO

which has a wave shape that varies as the output level changes. With tremolo the output wave shape is unaffected apart from variations in amplitude. Tremolo is a much more simple effect, which gives a much more simple sound than two VCOs. It is a useful feature for a synthesizer, especially a single VCO type, but it is no substitute for a second VCO.

With a very flexible synthesizer it might be possible to use the VCO for other forms of modulation. Probably the most useful of these is the ability to mix the low frequency oscillator's output into the control signal for the VCF. Especially when used with the VCF set for a high resonance level, this can provide some very interesting effects. With a suitable VCF both waa-waa and phaser type effects can be obtained.

Ring modulation

Ring modulation is an important form of modulation that enables metallic sounds to be generated. As explained in Chapter 1, instruments such as bells and gongs have two or three dimensional resonators that generate strong output signals at non-harmonically related frequencies. These non-harmonically related frequencies cannot be produced using a basic single VCO synthesizer. With a two VCO type it is certainly possible to offset the pitch of one oscillator from the other so that frequencies which are not harmonically related to one oscillator are generated by the other. This does not give the required effect though, as the spectrum of frequencies on the output is far too simple. You have what is really just two notes plus their harmonics, and a simple harmony. Gongs and bells produce complex output signals that contain complex harmonies.

Ring modulation requires two VCOs, and their output signals are mixed in a way that provides a complex output signal. A proper ring modulator provides double balancing, which means that neither of the input signals appear at the output. In practice there is usually significant breakthrough of at least one signal at the output, but this is not necessarily a bad thing. There may be a balance control that enables the degree of breakthrough to be adjusted, or (more probably) a control to set the amount of ring modulation signal that is mixed with the direct output of the VCOs.

Sum and difference signals
The main output signals from a ring modulator are the sum and difference signals. The mathematics involved here are delightfully simple. Assume that the VCOs are operating at 440Hz and 660Hz. The sum frequency is (as one would probably expect) the sum of these two frequencies, or 1100Hz in other words. The difference frequency is the higher input frequency minus the lower one, or 220Hz in this case. With these example figures the sum frequency is not harmonically related to either of the input frequencies. The 220Hz signal is half one of the input frequencies, and is what I suppose could be termed a sub-harmonic. With one oscillator set 50% higher in frequency (i.e. tuned a fifth higher) quite a pleasant effect is obtained. In practice the tuning of one oscillator is usually offset very slightly from the correct frequency so that a low frequency beat note is obtained.

Of course, ring modulation is not normally used with pure sinewaves, and there would be a number of input frequencies at each input. This gives a complex output signal containing a large number of frequency components. Fig.2.16 shows a simple example. Even with two input signals that each consist of just the fundamental and second harmonic, this still gives many new frequencies. It is not essential to use a separation of a fifth, and some other musical intervals provide good musical sounds. Using

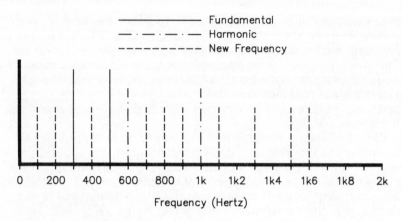

Figure 2.16 Even two simple input signals generate a number of new frequencies when ring modulated

the wrong frequencies can give very discordant results indeed, if you like that type of thing!

An important point to note is that the output from a ring modulator does not contain the two input frequencies, and the notes you play on the keyboard are not the ones that emerge from the modulator. This effect is more usable if the ring modulation signal is used to enrich the direct output from the VCOs, rather than being used as the sole output signal.

I am not entirely sure how the name 'ring' modulation was derived. The most likely explanation is that the name refers to the fact that it produces ringing type sounds.

More modulation

Other types of modulation are possible, but they are not available on many instruments. They can provide some interesting effects, but not what everyone would consider to be musical results. One possibility is to use a second VCO in place of the low frequency oscillator when modulating the VCO, VCA or VCF. This can produce some complex output signals, and if you have an instrument that can use a VCO to modulate the VCF it is certainly worth giving it a try.

Pulse width modulation

An interesting form of modulation is the pulse width type. This is used with a variable pulse waveform, but the pulse width is controlled via a control voltage rather than using a front panel control. Fig.2.17 shows the way in which this form of modulation

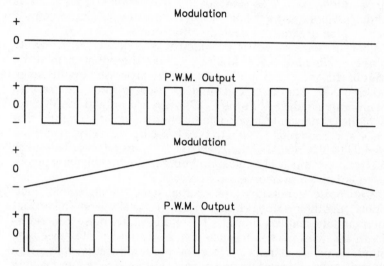

Figure 2.17 Example pulse width modulation waveforms

operates. In the top pair of waveforms the modulation voltage is constant at zero, and the modulated output signal is a square wave having a 1 to 1 mark-space ratio. In other words, the positive ('mark') period is equal to the negative ('space') period. In the lower pair of waveforms the modulation signal is a low frequency triangular signal. Where this signal passes through zero volts, the modulated signal is still a squarewave. However, when it is at a higher voltage the mark-space ratio is increased, and when it is at a lower voltage this ratio is decreased.

The effect of pulse width modulation is similar to a swept highpass filter. Remember that the strength of the fundamental and lower order harmonics varies with the pulse width. Quite interesting effects can be obtained using either a low frequency oscillator or an envelope generator as the modulation source.

Big noise

A noise generator is something that is absent from many analogue synthesizers, but in my opinion this is a pretty huge omission. While it is true that few sounds are totally noise based, a lot of sounds have a significant noise content. Using a noise generator as the sole signal source it is possible to produce wind and rain type sounds, as well as some useful percussion sounds such as handclaps. Some added noise can give greater realism to sounds such as pipe organs and bowed string sounds.

Where a noise source is provided it is generally of the white noise type. Its output should be mixed into the signal chain at the input of the VCA, and it will therefore be processed by this stage and the VCF. The latter can then be used to filter the noise to obtain other shades. With the VCOs switched off and the VCF set for high resonance, it is possible to filter the noise so tightly that it has apparent pitch. With the VCF set up correctly, it is then possible to play notes on the keyboard in the usual way. This gives an effect very much like the sound obtained when blowing across the top of an empty bottle, or a pipe.

Most noise generators are of the standard electronic 'hiss' variety, and their output voltage varies in a totally random fashion. There are alternatives though. There are digital noise generators of various types, some of which give a standard white noise type sound. Some are extremely basic and provide what is really just a series of pulses of random width and random separation. Fig.2.18 shows the type of waveform generated by a device of this type. This still gives a hissing sound, but one which in practice normally has a rather low pitch and which has a very rough sound in comparison to white noise. This can be useful for explosive sound effects, but is not very good for synthesizing most noise based musical instrument sounds.

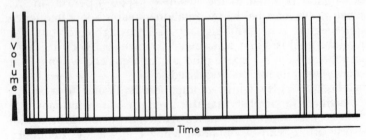

Figure 2.18 The simple form of noise signal generated by some digital noise circuits

Another method of generating a noise signal is to ring modulate two signals, then ring modulate the resultant signal with the output of another oscillator, and so on. The number of oscillators and modulators used depends on the type of noise that is required. Using more than about six stages gives such a complex output signal containing so many frequencies that it is virtually indistinguishable from a white noise signal. Using a lower number gives a sort of metallic noise which is very good for synthesizing cymbal type sounds. Apart from sampled cymbal sounds, this method of synthesis gives the most convincing cymbal sounds I have heard.

Dual resonance

A highly desirable but rare feature is a dual resonance filter. This provides a double peaked response of the type shown in Fig.2.19.

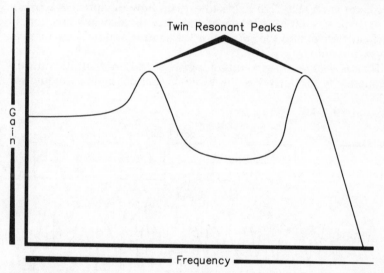

Figure 2.19 Dual resonance gives two peaks in the frequency response and some interesting effects

The human vocal cavity has twin resonances, and this type of response is supposed to be good for producing voice sounds. It can produce some other quite interesting and useful effects as well. In some cases the higher peak is fixed at one octave above the main one, but in other cases it is possible to adjust the separation of the two peaks in the response.

Sample and hold

This is another rare and relatively little used facility, but one which can provide some interesting effects. It is used to generate a sort of random low frequency oscillator signal. It is often regarded as a low frequency noise generator, although this description is not entirely accurate.

We have already encountered a sample and hold circuit in the keyboard section of a synthesizer. The sample and hold circuit used in this application is similar, but the voltage it is 'remembering' is one provided by a VCO or a noise generator. The low frequency oscillator provides a control signal, and the sampling of the input signal occurs once per low frequency oscillator cycle. Whatever the voltage obtained from the VCO or noise generator at the instant the sample and hold circuit is triggered by the low frequency oscillator, that voltage is held for one low frequency oscillator cycle. Fig.2.20 helps to explain how this process works. Here a new sample is taken at the start of each low frequency oscillator cycle, and the source for the sample and hold circuit is a noise generator.

This is not a truly random noise signal in that its output frequency is fixed, and is the same as that of the low frequency

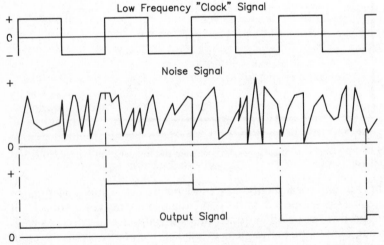

Figure 2.20 Using a sample and hold circuit to generate a sort of low frequency noise signal

oscillator. This gives modulation provided by a sample and hold circuit the all important rhythmic quality. It is random in that the output voltage (and hence the depth of modulation obtained) is quite unpredictable.

Portamento

This is a simple and virtually standard feature for an analogue synthesizer. It is also known as 'glide', and it simply means having a steady change in pitch from one note to the next rather than almost instant jumps in pitch. Certain acoustic instruments can provide the same effect, including fretless string instruments such as violins and cellos (i.e. glissando). Portamento is therefore needed in order to permit a faithful synthesis of these instruments when this playing style is used.

Ideally there should be a portamento rate control, and this simply controls the time taken for the pitch to glide over a certain range of notes. The glide rate normally has to be reasonably fast or you will tend to find that you have moved onto the next note before the previous one has reached the right pitch.

A practical synthesizer

The exact facilities available on a synthesizer vary substantially from one instrument to another. A typical instrument would have an arrangement along the lines of Fig.2.21. The basic signal sources are two VCOs and a noise generator. These are fed to a mixer and each one can be switched on or off. In most cases the level of each signal source would be continuously adjustable from zero to full output. This is particularly important in the case of the noise generator. This will most often be used to add a relatively small amount of background noise to the main signal provided by one or both VCOs. It must be critically adjusted in order to obtain the desired effect. The VCOs will each have several waveforms available, possibly including a variable pulse type. It is more than a little useful if the outputs of the VCOs can be ring modulated rather than just mixed.

There are no controls for the VCA, but this is controlled via its envelope generator and what are normally the attack, decay, sustain and release knobs. It is very useful (but rare) to have a separate envelope shaper for the noise generator. For some types

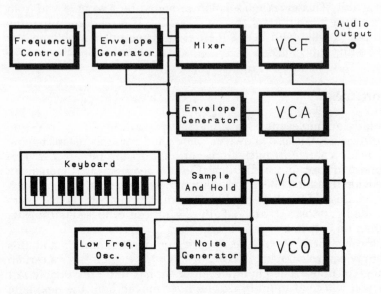

Figure 2.21 A typical synthesizer configuration

of sound the noise is only needed during part of the sound. An example of this would be a bowed string sound, where there is usually proportionately more noise during the attack stage than later in the envelope. The VCF is controlled in a similar manner, but it can additionally be fed with the keyboard voltage. A frequency control enables the range of frequencies covered to be shifted up or down so that the desired overall level of filtering can be obtained.

A low frequency oscillator is available for modulation purposes, and this gives vibrato if it is used to modulate the VCO. Its frequency should be variable, and there should also be a 'depth' control to enable the degree of modulation to be varied over wide limits. The low frequency oscillator will be of limited use unless it is possible to direct its output to other parts of the synthesizer. The modulation facilities are something that really do vary enormously from one instrument to another. In the early days, synthesizers were in a modular form, with all inputs and outputs brought out to sockets on the front panel. You could then connect any output to any input via a 'patch' lead. The term 'patch' is still used today, but everything is generally under the control of switches. This is much neater and more convenient of course, but it can limit the range of sounds that can be produced. It can be particularly restrictive with regard to modulation where some instruments provide for only the most basic forms. Other instruments are very good though, and can provide every form of modulation that could be usefully applied to their circuits.

With a synthesizer consisting of a number of basic building blocks with each one having about three or four controls, inevitably there are a large number of controls to contend with. Do not panic at the sight of all these controls — they are not too difficult to tame if you understand the basic make up of the instrument. The instrument's manual should contain a diagram which shows the particular circuit blocks that are present, the ways in which they can be patched together, and the controls that apply to each part of the instrument. When you set up a synthesizer take one section of the instrument at a time rather than adjusting the controls in an arbitrary fashion. At least, take things one stage at a time initially. When you have things set up in a way that gives a sound very close to the desired one, you may then need to do some relatively impulsive adjusting in order to 'fine tune' the sound.

Setting up your own sounds

So much for the facilities available on an analogue synthesizer — how is it set up to produce various types of sound? If you have access to an analogue synthesizer with its rows of controls and numerous switches you can learn a great deal about synthesis by playing around with various control settings for a few hours. Modern polyphonic synthesizers with their multi-timbral capabilities are a definite advance on the old monophonic instruments, but their push buttons and LED/LCD displays make adjustments to their sound generator circuits a relatively slow and tedious task. They are certainly less than ideal for learning about synthesis. They are a lot better than nothing though, and ultimately you can only learn the art of sound synthesis by trying to synthesize sounds. Some modern synthesizers have add-on control boxes available, and these are a decided asset if you are going to undertake more than a small amount of sound programming.

Use your ears
A good starting point is to try listening to a range of instruments, and attempt to analyze their sounds. Do they jump almost

immediately to a high level (like a piano or a guitar), or does the sound build up a little more slowly (like most woodwind instruments)? After the attack period does the sound decay quickly, decay slowly, or sustain before entering the decay period? Does the sound seem to be reasonably pure, or is it obviously rich in harmonics? How does the character of the sound change as its envelope progresses? Is there an obvious noise content, or non-harmonic components in the sound?

Ideally you would have electronic test and measuring equipment in order to provide all the answers, but equipment of this type is difficult to obtain, and for the vast majority of amateur users is prohibitively expensive. You therefore have to rely on what your ears can tell you, and in due course on the experience you have gained.

Analyze the envelope

Probably the easiest aspect of a sound to analyze by ear is its envelope. With the more sluggish sounds you should have no difficulty in hearing how the sound rises and falls in volume. Draw out the apparent envelope shape. Human hearing tends to compress sounds, and quite large changes in volume are heard as only moderate changes. Most synthesizer controls take this into account, but you will probably find initially that setting up the envelope generator for a particular shape does not give quite the effect you expected. Do not worry too much about this, and be prepared to do some fine adjustments in order to get things just right. You should soon become more familiar with the controls and find it easier to get the right settings, but the chances of getting everything just right at the first attempt will always be minimal!

Some 'envelope shapes are too fast for the rises and falls in volume to be heard as such, or there are parts of the envelope that change too rapidly for the human ear to perceive them properly. Some intelligent guessing will usually reveal the approximate envelope shape. With a brief 'ping' of sound it is clear that the attack and decay times are both quite short. If a sound starts with a 'ping' but then sustains for some time, this would suggest that the attack and decay controls should both be set for quite short times, with the sustain set at a moderate level. If a sound cuts off abruptly, then clearly a short release control setting is required.

With an ADSR envelope generator the sustain and release phases may not be required. Setting both controls at zero will effectively eliminate these phases, and the envelope shape can then be controlled using the attack and decay controls. If the decay phase is not needed, set the decay control at zero and the sustain level at maximum. When the envelope reaches the end of the attack time it will remain at full volume until the key is released. It then enters the release phase. This gives what is effectively an attack/decay envelope shaper.

Harmonics

Judging the particular harmonics present in a signal, how strong they are, and how they change during the course of the sound, is a much more difficult business. Presumably anyone who is interested in sound synthesis will also be reasonably musical, and will have a well developed sense of hearing. With a well developed sense of hearing it is not too difficult to judge whether a sound has a fairly high level of purity or is rich in harmonics (or somewhere between the two). You may even find that on a steady signal you can pick out the individual frequency components. This is much more difficult on a sound of changing timbre, and most musical sounds fall into this category.

This is something where experience is certainly a very big advantage, and you may have to accept that things will be a struggle at first. If a sound is clearly of quite high purity and has only a weak harmonic content, then a triangular waveform with its low harmonic content is the obvious starting point. The method of synthesis used in a conventional analogue synthesizer is known as 'subtractive' synthesis. The reason for this is that the main signal processing stages of the instrument (the VCA and VCF) cannot add any new frequencies to the signal. The VCF is used to remove or attenuate components on the basic output from the VCO or other signal sources. This is not of purely academic importance, and it is something that it is crucial to keep in mind. The basic output of the VCO or other signal sources must have all the frequency components that are needed on the final output signal, and at every stage of that signal. Not only must they be present, they must also be of adequate strength.

It has to be said that subtractive synthesis is a fairly crude way of handling the problem. There are better ways, but they are much more complicated and difficult to implement. For this reason there are still a lot of analogue symthesizers in use today, or more modern forms of synthesizer that still use what is really a form of subtractive synthesis. On the face of it, a waveform that has all the harmonics in abundance could be used as the basic signal for synthesizing any sound (apart from metallic or noise based types). In reality things are not as simple as this. The limitations of the

VCF must be taken into account. This may not be capable of producing a reasonably pure output from a signal that is rich in strong harmonics. Most VCFs will give quite a good sinewave by applying lowpass filtering to a triangular waveform. Few will give really good results on an input signal such as a pulse or sawtooth type. Even if the VCF can give acceptable results from an input signal that is rich in harmonics, the settings of the controls are likely to be far less critical if the synthesis is based on a sound that is closer to the one required as the final output.

Another point to bear in mind is that many synthesizers have a VCF that provides only lowpass filtering. If you require a thin sound having a weak fundamental you must use a pulse signal having a suitably narrow pulse width. A lowpass filter can only attenuate the harmonics relative to the fundamental. It cannot attenuate the fundamental frequency more than the harmonics. The exception to this is where a high resonance setting is used. It is then possible to accentuate one of the harmonics (or two with a dual resonant filter).

A further point to keep in mind is that many sounds do not contain all the harmonics. In many cases only the odd or even numbered harmonics are present, and a waveform having the correct harmonics must be used as the starting point.

Sounds close

Instead of starting from scratch when setting up a sound on a synthesizer, many synthesists prefer to find a set of parameters that are close to their requirements, and then do some fine tuning. Even quite experienced synthesists often find this to be a much quicker and easier route to the desired result, and it is almost certainly the best approach for beginners to adopt, where possible. Most modern synthesizers have a number of ready-programmed sounds that are available at the press of a few buttons. It should not take long to go through these and find the one with the sound that is closest to the one you require.

With older analogue synthesizers there are no sound data memories, and the sound you get is the one dictated by the control settings. This is good in that you can instantly adjust any parameter. It is very easy to make adjustments to an instrument of this type, and you soon become familiar with it. Setting up a modern push-button controlled synthesizer is a much more convoluted task. The drawback is that the factory preset sounds are in the form of sets of parameters on charts in the manual, and every parameter must be entered by hand! The names given to the sounds should give you a good idea of what to expect, so that only a few of the more likely ones need to be tried. Unfortunately, some of the names used can be a trifle fanciful.

Generalizations

In order to obtain a desired sound it normally requires all the controls to be set up very accurately. On the other hand, there are some generalizations that can help to get you off to a good start. These are particularly useful if, for some reason, you cannot use the method of modifying an existing sound, as described above.

Pulse waveform

If an acoustic instrument has a small resonator it will usually produce a rather thin sound. The smaller the resonator relative to the pitch range of the instrument, the thinner the sound is likely to be. Oboe, electric piano, koto, and sitar are all good examples of instruments which produce this type of sound. The basic waveform for this type of sound is a pulse type, which contains a weak fundamental signal, and all harmonics. Obviously, if you have a synthesizer with a variable pulse width, some fine adjusting of the waveform can be used to optimize the quality of the synthesis. An oboe sound, for example, requires a greater pulse width than a sitar sound. Highpass filtering can also be used to give thin sounds, but you then lose the ability to attenuate the higher harmonics.

Sawtooth waveform

The sawtooth or ramp waveform is another one which contains all harmonics, but it has a stronger fundamental content than does a narrow pulse signal. This type of waveform is used for synthesizing a number of instrument sounds, including many string and brass types. These may not seem to be very similar, but they are both quite 'bright' sounds. The main difference is that a brass instrument has a sharper attack phase, and is usually that much brighter. If you sample a brass sound, alter its envelope and apply some lowpass filtering you can usually produce a quite passable string sound!

51

Squarewave

A squarewave is another bright sound, but it is markedly different from pulse and sawtooth sounds. Remember that only the odd numbered harmonics are present. This is another waveform that is used for synthesizing many instruments. Some examples would be clarinet, organ and harp.

Triangular waveform

A triangular waveform is effectively a less bright squarewave, and applying heavy lowpass filtering to a squarewave will give you a signal that has a more or less triangular shape. A triangular wave is suitable for the same kinds of sound as a squarewave, but only the less bright types. This includes such things as flute, recorder and whistle sounds. With these sounds you have the choice of using a triangular wave or a heavily filtered squarewave. The triangular wave is probably the better option, especially if the synthesizer lacks high slope (24dB per octave or more) filters. Bear in mind though, that many sounds which have quite high purity are relatively harsh during the attack period. A triangular waveform would probably not permit accurate synthesis of the attack phase with sounds of this type.

Sinewave

A sinewave is not much used in subtractive synthesis because very few instruments can be synthesized using this waveform. Remember that a filtered sinewave is still a sinewave, and this waveform lacks versatility when applied to subtractive synthesis. A sinewave plus a small amount of added noise can produce a reasonable flute sound, but not much else.

Noise

Noise is little used as the main signal source, and is more useful in small amounts for making subtle differences to sounds that can really add to their realism. Apart from flute sounds, it can be used to good effect with sounds such as pipe organs and drums. It can be used as the sole signal source with sounds such as handclaps, jet roars, etc.

Table 2.1 summarizes this information, and should be useful for quick reference purposes.

Table 2.1 Basic waveforms for synthesis

Waveform	Harmonics	Instruments
Pulse	All (weak fundamental)	Oboe, electric piano, some acoustic pianos, koto, sitar, vibraphone
Sawtooth	All	Strings, brass, guitar, harmonica
Square	Odd order	Clarinet, organ, harp, recorder
Triangle	Odd order (weak)	Flute, recorder, whistles
Sinewave	None	Flute, pan flute
Noise	Not applicable	Wind and rain, handclap, blown pipes, jet roar
Added noise	Not applicable	Flute, pan flute, pipe organ

Multiple waves

Where you have either more than one waveform available at once, or two VCOs, or possibly both, getting the right combination can be more difficult. Virtually all synthesized sounds are much more lifelike using some form of multiple wave source, and preferably two VCOs. The easy approach is to try getting things as close as possible using one VCO and one waveform, and then try experimenting a little in an attempt to improve matters. With relatively simple sounds such as flutes you may get quite good results using a single VCO, but even with these sounds a second VCO can sometimes make a worthwhile difference. With the more simple sounds the second VCO is almost invariably used at a relatively low level.

For more complex sounds the use of two VCOs is mandatory. Some quite good organ sounds can be obtained using a single VCO, but they do not really compare with twin VCO equivalents. The ability to set one VCO an octave higher than the other is a standard feature, and an extremely useful one. This effectively boosts certain harmonics of the lower frequency oscillator, or adds harmonics that are not present on this signal. In particular, the second harmonic is strongly boosted by the fundamental of the higher frequency signal. This technique can be used to good effect with a wide range of sounds. These include such instruments as harpsichords, certain types of organ, xylophones, electric pianos, guitars, woodwind, and steel drums. In many cases it is advantageous if the two oscillators can be set two or more octaves apart, and to any note rather than just full octaves higher. This permits any harmonic within reason to be boosted by the fundamental of the higher frequency oscillator. Most synthesizers can accommodate this method of operation. Fractionally detuning the higher frequency oscillator produces a very rich effect which substantially enhances most sounds.

Brass and string sounds are generally better with the two oscillators set to the same octave. Slight detuning of one oscillator gives a simple ensemble effect and is much used with both string and brass sounds.

Ring modulation is, of course, required for metallic sounds. It is mostly used with the two VCOs one or more octaves apart and on different notes. Slight detuning of one oscillator to produce a low frequency beat note is usually necessary in order to give the right effect. Waveforms that are rich in harmonics generally give the best results. It would be a mistake to think of ring modulation as only useful for metallic sounds. This is its primary function, but if used in moderation it can be used to good effect when synthesizing many types of instrument. These include harp, guitar, saxophone, and koto.

Filtering

You are unlikely to find a waveform that is perfect for a given sound, and at least a little help from the VCF will normally be needed. The nature of the sound produced by many instruments changes quite dramatically over their sound compass. With some aspects of the sound you may have to accept a compromise. The envelope shape is perhaps the best example of this. Consider a piano, where at the low pitch end of its range notes can be sustained for several seconds. This contrasts with the rather pathetic 'plink' sound produced by most pianos when their highest notes are played. With most synthesizers there is no way of varying the envelope shape with the pitch of the note, and the best compromise settings have to be sought. Playing the high notes with the briefest of key presses can also help to optimize the accuracy of the synthesis. With some synthesizers a form of split keyboard operation is possible, and a different series of settings can then be used on the high and low notes of the instrument. You need to be very careful with any keyboard split of this type though, as the split can sometimes be very obvious when the instrument is played.

The VCF offers one way of trying to get the right sound over a wide frequency range. It is probably best to get the sound as accurate as possible at a frequency somewhere in the middle of the compass over which the sound will be used, and then try adjusting the keyboard and envelope amounts to optimize results over the entire pitch range. This is largely a matter of homing in on the right settings by trial and error.

Most acoustic instruments have a string or other resonator that produces the basic sound, and a hollow body (e.g. violin and guitar) which provides a sort of mechanical filtering by accentuating some frequencies and absorbing others. Using two oscillators with one boosting certain harmonics of the other is one means of electronically mimicking this. Another is to use the VCF with moderate resonance. Many sounds can be improved by advancing the resonance control a little, but try not to get carried away. Some very lively sounds can be produced, but they are not necessarily particularly accurate representations of the instrument being synthesized, and may quickly become wearing to listen to.

Resonance is very important with noise based sounds which rarely (if ever) use straightforward white noise. In the majority of cases a high resonance setting is needed. A moderate setting is adequate for wind and rain type sounds, but handclaps, cymbals and a lot of other noise based sounds require something approaching maximum resonance.

LFO

A low frequency oscillator can be used for several types of modulation, but only vibrato is used to any extent when synthesizing acoustic instrument sounds. Most sounds can be improved by the addition of small amounts of vibrato, but you should not get carried away with this effect. Many acoustic instruments can be played in such a way that strong vibrato is produced, but it would be a mistake artistically to habitually play them in that way. Vibrato can be used to good effect with sounds such as strings, brass, organs and woodwind, but it does not work well with all sounds. Plucked or hammered string sounds (harp, harpsichord, piano, etc.) are generally better without this effect.

Playing style

Getting a good synthesized sound is only half the battle won. Playing style is important, and it is also something that it may be difficult to get right. Most musicians are only able to play one, or perhaps two different types of instrument. With a synthesizer you effectively have hundreds of different instruments at your disposal. Unless you have a synthesizer that can be controlled via some other form of controller (such as a guitar or breath controller), all these instruments will be played from the keyboard, regardless of how they are normally played.

Listening to a recording of an instrument being played can be very instructive, and watching and listening to a live performance can be even more helpful. Being realistic about it, with a lot of synthesizers, especially the less expensive and older types, there is limited scope fo playing in a way that accurately reflects the sound of the real thing. Unfortunately, a lot of synthesizers are not even touch sensitive, and you do not have any control whatever over the dynamics. Fortunately, touch sensitivity does now seem to be included on many of the cheaper synthesizers that have been recently introduced. Where touch sensitivity is lacking, it is important to get the optimum settings for the envelope shapers, particularly in the attack phase.

With some instruments (many string types for example) the player normally introduces some vibrato on sustained notes. Some synthesizers can cater for this by having a delay on the modulation, so that it is only produced on notes of more than a certain duration. Without this feature you may have to settle for vibrato on all notes. The alternative is to switch off the LFO and introduce the vibrato manually using the pitch wheel, which is not as easy as it sounds.

Aftertouch has been a very rare feature in the past, but it is now a standard feature on up-market equipment as well as a few lower cost instruments. This gives some control over the dynamics after the initial attack period. With instruments such as string and wind types the player has a large degree of control over the envelope shape. The volume can be raised or lowered at will at any stage of the envelope. In theory, aftertouch affords the keyboard player the same facility by pressing more or less hard on the keys. In practice aftertouch seems to be much better implemented on some instruments than others. If the degree of aftertouch is adjustable it is worth taking some time to get this parameter set at a level where you find it easy to control the volume properly. Even if it is not brilliantly implemented, aftertouch is always a worthwhile feature, as is anything that gives you more control over the sound of the instrument.

A point worth mentioning is that polyphonic instruments often have a 'solo' or 'mono' switch. This affects the way in which the envelope generator behaves, and if you are synthesizing a monophonic instrument (woodwind, brass, etc.) this switch should be activated. Fig.2.22 shows the difference when the solo

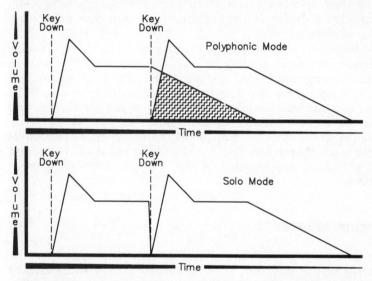

Figure 2.22 Solo mode can give better results when synthesizing some monophonic instruments

mode is used. When this mode is not used, playing a second note does not result in the first one being cut off. Existing notes will be cut short only when the instrument runs out of voices, which would typically be after note number eight was played. Clearly, instruments such as oboes and clarinets never provide more than one note at a time. With the instrument in the solo mode, it is effectively downgraded to a monophonic type, and each new note terminates the previous one, giving the desired effect. Of course, if the envelope is one which has a very short release period, selecting the solo mode will make very little difference. Once a key is released, that note will be almost immediately terminated anyway. Its only effect would be to ensure that you could not accidentally play more than one note at a time.

There is a potential problem which is a sort of inverse of the one described above. Sometimes a monophonic instrument fails to give the right effect when there only seems to be a need for one note at a time. Consider the case of a synthesized harp. By plucking several strings in rapid succession on a real harp you are only playing one note at a time. However, unlike a woodwind instrument, playing a new note does not automatically terminate the previous one. A rapid run along the strings of a harp could easily result in more than a dozen notes playing simultaneously. Even some polyphonic instruments would be unable to simulate this properly.

Some instruments provide a complication in the form of totally different sounds depending on how they are played. Bowed or plucked strings are a good example of this. The only way around this is to set up the two sounds and then switch from one to the other as required. Most modern synthesizers can handle this, and a few have provision for changing sounds with the aid of a foot-pedal. With the older instruments this sort of thing is not possible as there are no memory circuits to store sound data. The sound you get is the one dictated by the settings of the front panel controls.

Original sounds

So far we have only considered synthesizers in the role of pseudo-acoustic instruments, but there is no need to copy the sounds of conventional instruments at all. Synthesizers open up the possibility of producing sounds that are totally unlike any acoustic instrument, but which have tremendous musical potential. If you can imagine a sound then you should be able to get reasonably close to it using any good synthesizer. The techniques are much the same as for real instrument sounds.

You do not need to have a specific sound in mind. Trying random control settings is a perfectly valid approach to developing new sounds. If you find a sound that is quite interesting and has musical possibilities, try some fine adjustments to see if you can improve it. If your synthesizer supports some of the more unusual forms of modulation, try adding some of these to conventional instrument sounds. Modulating the VCF and adding noise to signals can produce some good space type sounds.

When striving for original synthesized sounds there is perhaps a temptation to search for the more way-out ones. These can certainly be used to good effect, but are probably not the most useful. The so-called 'impressionistic' sounds are almost certainly the most valuable original sounds. If you listen to synthesized music you will soon hear sounds that are like strings, brass, etc., and used in much the same way. They are not really accurate representations of real strings, brass, etc., and do not set out to be. They are purely electronic sounds that fulfil the same function as their acoustic counterparts, and in essence are the same as these instruments. Hence the term impressionistic. If you study the preset sounds of some synthesizers you will find examples of these sounds under such names as 'Synth Strings', 'Synth Bass', etc.

Finally

Whatever type of sound you are trying to synthesize, be prepared to take some time to get things just right. With so many parameters under your control it would be unreasonable to expect new sounds to be perfected in a couple of minutes. Above all, be prepared to experiment.

3 Modern synthesis

There are a surprisingly large number of different techniques used in modern synthesizers. Some of these are really just variations on conventional analogue synthesis, but others are based on totally different methods of signal generation. In this chapter we will look at several of the more important methods of modern sound synthesis, including PD (phase distortion) and FM (frequency modulation), which seem to have dominated the synthesizer world in recent years.

Digital waves

Probably the most fundamental difference between modern synthesizers and earlier ones is that modern instruments use what are largely digital circuits. Analogue synthesizers, despite their name, are not necessarily devoid of any digital circuits. They are analogue in the sense that their sound generating circuits use analogue circuits, such as filters and amplifiers. Any digital circuitry would usually be confined to the keyboard circuit, and possibly some control circuits such as the ones which route signals to various parts of the instrument.

As instruments became more sophisticated, digital circuits began to play an increasingly important role. In order to control everything properly in a polyphonic instrument, a microprocessor control circuit was virtually mandatory. Analogue circuits can be controlled from a microprocessor using digital to analogue converters, and a number of synthesizers are effectively conventional analogue instruments controlled from digital circuits via suitable converters. This is in many respects doing things the hard way, and there is an obvious benefit in using digital sound generator circuits that are easily controlled using a microprocessor. Most manufacturers seem to have opted for a minimal amount of analogue circuitry in their instruments.

In many synthesizers the VCOs, VCFs and VCAs are replaced by DCOs, DCFs and DCAs. In other words, they use digitally controlled oscillators, filters and amplifiers, instead of conventional voltage controlled devices. These digital versions of the basic synthesizer building blocks are in some cases just conventional circuits plus converters, while in others they are truly digital circuits. In many instruments a mixture of the two types are utilized.

These days a DCO is almost invariably a fully digital circuit rather than an ordinary oscillator plus digital converter. Most DCOs are quite complex circuits that are not oscillators in the conventional sense, but are what would be more accurately termed digital waveform synthesizers. Apart from easy digital control, the main advantage of a circuit of this type is that it can produce a wide range of waveforms. In fact any waveform at all can be produced using this type of signal source. This contrasts with ordinary oscillators where it is difficult to produce anything other than a few basic waveforms such as sine, pulse and sawtooth types. Conventional subtractive synthesis relies very heavily on the mixing of waveforms and filtering to give a suitable basic waveform. This system is not used as a matter of choice — it is the only simple method possible with analogue circuits. With a DCO you can simply generate whatever basic waveform you require.

The waveform diagram of Fig.3.1 helps to show the basic way in which a DCO functions. The required waveform is held in an electronic memory circuit called a ROM (read only memory). It is

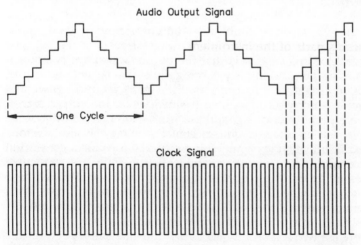

Figure 3.1 A DCO operates by repeatedly outputting a series of voltages

held in the form of a series of numbers which represent the amplitude of the signal at regular intervals during the course of the wave. In this example the waveform is a triangular type. If the initial value is 0 and the next one is 10, then subsequent values would be 20, 30, 40, etc. The numbers would continue to rise in this way until the peak value was reached, and then they would decrement ten at a time until the end of the waveform was reached at a value of 0 again.

The values held in the ROM are read in sequence at a rate controlled by a clock oscillator. At the beginning of each clock cycle the next value is read from ROM, and the read values are fed to a digital to analogue converter circuit that provides corresponding output voltages. When a full set of values has been read and one complete cycle has been produced, the process is repeated to generate the next cycle, then repeated again, and so on. The frequency of the output signal is proportional to the frequency of the clock oscillator. To raise the pitch of the output signal by one octave, for example, it would merely be necessary to double the frequency of the clock signal. If obtaining a certain pitch requires an impractically high clock frequency, missing out alternate values will increase the output frequency by an octave for any given clock frequency. By missing out more values the output frequency can be boosted by two or three octaves if necessary.

Resolution

This system gives a continuous output signal of controllable frequency and having the right waveform, or does it? The drawback of this system is that the output waveform is stepped rather than the continuously varying signal that is generated by an analogue circuit. These steps in the signal produce unwanted harmonics and other unwanted frequencies on the output signal. With a high frequency signal these will be too high in pitch to be audible, but on a low frequency signal they may be very obvious indeed. With suitable circuits this method of waveform generation can certainly be very successful. Most people are extremely impressed by the audio quality of compact disc players, and these produce a digitized output signal complete with steps. With inadequate circuits the quality of the output signal will be too low to be of any practical use in synthesizer applications.

There are two important factors that must be met if good results are to be attained. One is simply that there must be a high clock frequency. This produces a large number of small steps in the waveform so that it is very close to the required wave shape and has very low distortion levels. Allied to this is the resolution of the system. A digital system has finite resolution, and it cannot produce *any* desired voltage. The waveform might dictate an output voltage of 1.2345 volts, but the circuit might have an output that increments in (say) 0.1 volt steps. The choice would therefore be between 1.2 or 1.3 volts, and a significant error would have to be accepted in either case. Apart from this error, there is the problem that with a high clock rate and low resolution there would often be no change in value from one clock cycle to the next. This would effectively reduce the clock frequency and give poor results.

With a clock frequency of around 30kHz or more, and tens of thousands of different output voltages available, excellent output quality can be achieved. With a clock rate of just a few thousand per second and a few hundred different output voltages available, results will be very much less impressive. It is worth noting that in modern synthesizers many of the controls are digital types. Instead of having a control knob with an infinite number of positions, push buttons or some form of stepped rotary control are used to select one of perhaps sixty-four available settings. Good resolution is equally important for control settings, but in most cases a few dozen settings are adequate. If you can hear little or no change from one setting to the next, the resolution of the control is perfectly adequate.

In the example waveform of Fig.3.1 a simple waveform is being synthesized. However, by having suitable values stored in the ROM it is possible to produce waveforms of any complexity. This method of synthesis is often termed 'wavetable' synthesis, because the available waveforms are in the form of tables of numbers stored in ROM.

With a range of suitable waveforms available it is certainly possible to produce some impressive sounds, but this is not a complete solution to sound synthesis. The waveform is constant from the beginning to the end of the sound. Twin DCOs and filtering are needed in order to produce complex sounds and changes in timbre during the course of each envelope. Some impressive sounds can be obtained using this system, which is essentially the system used in the Ensoniq ESQ-1 and a number of other instruments. There are variations on this basic scheme of things, and some instruments have the ability to 'crossfade' from one waveform to another. Thus you could, for example, have one waveform for the attack part of a sound, and then fade to another one for the rest of its duration. The impressive Roland SAS (structured adaptive synthesis) pianos take this a stage further and apparently use different wavetables depending on the velocity values read from the keyboard.

Synthesizers which use any system of the wavetable type should pose few problems for someone who is familiar with conventional analogue synthesis techniques. In most cases these instruments can be regarded as conventional analogue instruments having a highly sophisticated VCO section. It is important to listen to all the available waveforms as in many cases these have very different sounds to the usual square, triangle, pulse and sawtooth waves (although these old favourites are usually included as well). It is also worthwhile exploring any crossfade facility or any similar refinements. These can give some useful effects that no analogue synthesizer can provide.

LA synthesis

Linear arithmetic (LA) synthesis is the system used in a number of popular Roland instruments, such as the D-50, MT32, and D-110. This is a very complex system of sound synthesis, but one which is reasonably straightforward as far as the programmer is concerned. It could be regarded as a cross between conventional analogue synthesis and sound sampling. We will not consider sound sampling in any detail here as it is covered in a separate chapter, but in essence it is very much like a digital oscillator. The main difference is that the ROM contains a large number of values that represent hundreds or even thousands of cycles, not just a single cycle. The values held in the ROM are, of course, normally obtained by digitizing the sound from a real instrument, rather than using calculated values. This is in fact a form of digital recording, but only very brief snippets of sound are recorded. Usually a sample lasts no more than about a second. However, by looping the sample (i.e. playing the last cycle or a number of cycles over and over again) the signal can be maintained indefinitely. It can then be processed by conventional DCFs and DCAs in order to give the appropriate release period and changes in timbre once into the looping part of the signal.

With LA synthesis a large number of samples are held in ROM. Some of these are looped while others are of the 'single-shot' variety. The latter are mostly percussion sounds where looping would be inappropriate. In LA terminology the most basic unit of sound is called a 'partial', and this can be either a sampled sound or a synthesizer sound generator (similar to a conventional synthesizer sound generator). Sounds need only use a single partial, but they are mostly made by combining two or four partials to produce a 'tone'.

Using several partials for each sound gives greater versatility and enables more complex signals to be generated, but there is a trade-off in that the number of notes that can be played simultaneously is reduced. Taking the Roland D-110 as an example, it is 32 note polyphonic using one partial per voice, 16 note polyphonic using two per voice, or 8 note polyphonic using 4 partials per voice. As far as I am aware, all the LA synthesizers are multi-timbral. In other words, they are not just polyphonic, but a number of different sounds can be played at once. Up to eight different sounds can be produced at once, and there is additionally a ninth part which gives access to a range of percussion sounds. You therefore have what is virtually eight synthesizers plus a drum machine squeezed into each LA synthesizer! In fact each section of a synthesizer of this type is sometimes referred to as a 'virtual' synthesizer. Instruments of this type are particularly popular for MIDI sequencing.

Partials
If we look at the two types of partial in more detail, they use the arrangements shown in Fig.3.2 (synthesizer) and Fig.3.3 (sampled). Roland refer to the sampled sounds as PCM types. PCM stands for 'pulse code modulation', and is the type of sampling used. The synthesizer partials have obvious similarities to a conventional analogue synthesizer. The inclusion of an envelope generator to control the pitch of the signal is not a standard analogue synthesizer feature, but it is far from uncommon in modern instruments. Apart from opening up the possibility of generating some interesting effects, some acoustic instruments have some slight variation in pitch, particularly at the beginning of each note. The TVF and TVA stages are the 'time variant filter' and 'time variant amplifier'. These are the equivalents of the VCF (lowpass mode) and VCA stages of an analogue synthesizer. The PCM partial lacks any filtering, but it does include the TVA.

Pairs of partials can be mixed in a variety of ways, including placing them one in each stereo channel, or ring modulating them. Stereo operation seems to be a standard feature on LA synthesizers, as does a quite impressive built-in digital reverberation unit. Few modern synthesizers seem to have a conventional ADSR

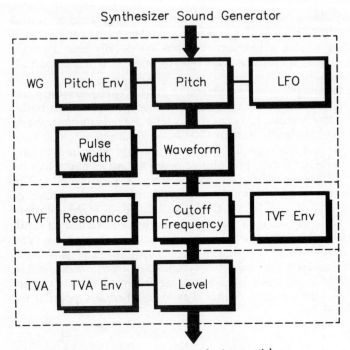

Figure 3.2 The stages used in an LA synthesizer partial

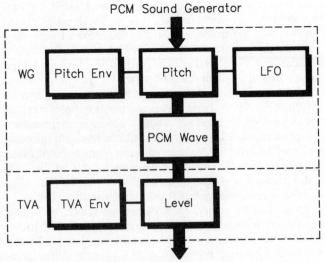

Figure 3.3 The make up of an LA PCM partial

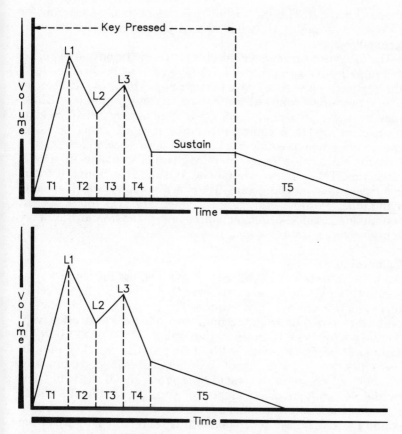

Figure 3.4 The LA envelope shapers are six stage types with optional sustain

envelope shaper. Most seem to include relatively complex envelope generators that can produce quite intricate envelope shapes. The LA synthesizers are no exception, and they use a multi-stage envelope generator of the type outlined in Fig.3.4. Apart from the fact that there is an extra stage in the envelope, it differs from a conventional ADSR type in that each stage is controlled by specifying an end level and a time to get to that level. The exception is the sustain phase which is comparable to the equivalent phase of an ADSR envelope generator. Note that the sustain period can be disabled so that the envelope shape is independent of the key being released (as in the lower envelope shape of Fig.3.4). This 'no sustain' mode is normally used only for percussion sounds, or what are 'rhythm tones' in Roland's terminology.

The LA synthesizers have the ability to vary the envelope period in sympathy with the pitch of the note played. High notes have shorter times—low notes have longer times. This is of most benefit when producing plucked or hammered string sounds. These roughly halve in duration for each doubling of pitch. Several degrees of envelope compression/stretching are available, so it should always be possible to obtain the desired effect.

There are a wide range of PCM sounds available in several categories. There are the rhythm sounds (such as bongo, various cymbals and handclap), and the attack sounds, which include xylophone, trumpet and clarinet. There are also the sustained sounds (such as cello, female voices and pianos), and the decay sounds (shot-1, shot-2, etc.).

Combining partials

An LA synthesizer could be used in more or less the same way as a conventional analogue synthesizer, but much of the power of this system lies in its PCM sounds. The initial part of a sound is often the most important section, and one which is often very complex with large changes in the timbre. Many of the best LA synthesis sounds are obtained by using a PCM attack sound for the initial part of the signal and a PCM sustained sound or synthesized signal for the rest of the sound. This is made possible by the versatile envelope shaper for each partial. Fig.3.5 shows how an attack sound (partial 1) can be merged with a sustained sound (partial 2) in order to obtain the desired effect. Apart from giving some excellent acoustic instrument sounds, this system is also well suited to the production of original and impressionistic sounds. Some unlikely combinations of partials can give some really excellent sounds.

This is another method of synthesis that should be quite easy to get on with provided you are familiar with conventional subtractive synthesis. The problem with LA synthesis, like most other modern approaches to sound synthesis, is that the programmer has to contend with a bewildering array of options. As with any synthesizer programming, it is a matter of taking things one stage at a time and not panicking at the thought of all those parameters. Having a vast range of control settings available certainly makes programming more difficult, but it is helpful to remember that it also provides tremendous sound making potential.

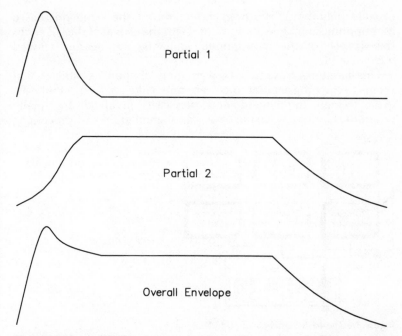

Figure 3.5 Many of the best LA sounds rely on this system of combining an attack sound with a sustained one

The obvious first step with LA synthesis is to select the main patch settings, such as the partials required, and how they will be combined. The more minor ones such as the reverberation type can be left until the final 'fine tuning' is carried out. Where LA departs most radically from conventional analogue synthesis is in the inclusion of its sampled sounds, and it is important to spend some time listening to these basic building blocks and becoming familiar with them. If you listen to the preset sounds of an LA instrument, or play one of the built-in multi-timbral demonstration pieces on an LA instrument that supports this feature, you will be left in no doubt about the potential of this system.

Phase distortion synthesis

I do not think that it would be an exaggeration to say that Casio's phase distortion (PD) method of sound synthesis has revolutionized the low cost end of the synthesizer market. It gave us quite capable polyphonic synthesizers at around the same price as a monophonic analogue instrument. With the arrival of the CZ series the demise of the monophonic analogue synthesizer seemed inevitable.

This is another example of a method of sound synthesis that seems to the programmer to be very much like analogue synthesis, even though the circuits and processes involved are totally different. Fig.3.6 shows the basic signal generation and processing

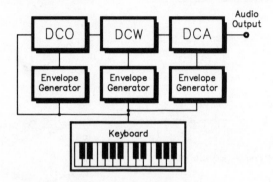

Figure 3.6 The basic signal chain in a PD synth

chain used in PD synthesis. This is highly simplified as it omits such things as the low frequency oscillator and the ability to mix the outputs of two signal chains (including ring modulating them if required).

Digital controlled wave
The basic signal is generated by a DCO, and this section of the unit includes an envelope generator that can 'bend' the pitch. At the output there is a DCA and envelope generator to provide envelope shaping of the output signal. The middle section of the signal chain is the DCW and its envelope generator. DCW stands for 'digital controlled wave', and this modifies the wave shape of the output signal. However, it does not do so using filtering. Its effect is very much the same as a lowpass filter, and it can be used in basically the same way. It is not a filter though, and this is something that needs to be kept in mind.

In Chapter 2 we saw how pulse width modulation can be used to alter the timbre of a sound, and give an effect that is similar to swept filtering. The DCW section of a PD synthesizer works in a manner which is much more like pulse width modulation than filtering. It relies on distorting the waveform at source in order to control its harmonic content. Pulse width modulation has limited potential as it will work only with simple pulse waveforms. The use of a DCO enables much more sophisticated waveform control to be achieved.

In Fig.3.7 the upper waveform in each pair represents a signal that controls the clock rate of the DCO, and the lower waveform

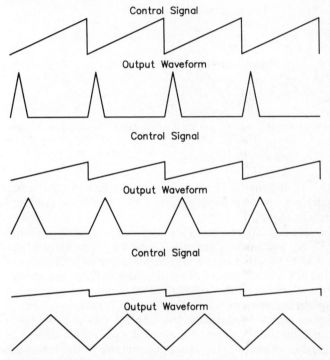

Figure 3.7 Varying the clock rate of a DCO gives considerable control over the output waveform

is that of the resultant output signal. In the upper set the control signal provides a constant clock frequency and at a rate which results in the full DCO cycle being produced. In the second pair of waveforms the clock rate is still constant, but it has been slowed down considerably. This results in less than the full DCO cycle being produced before the next cycle is commenced and the existing one is terminated. This stretches the initial part of the waveform so that it constitutes a complete cycle. In the third set

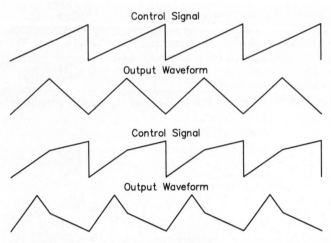

Figure 3.8 Using a changing clock frequency to phase distort the output waveform

of signals this stretching has been taken a stage further, and what was originally a form of pulsed output signal has been changed into a triangular signal.

Even just slowing down the clock and not outputting all the values in ROM provides quite good control over the output waveform. The PD system uses a somewhat more refined method though. With PD synthesis the full set of values in ROM are always used, but the clock does not operate at a constant rate. Fig.3.8 helps to explain the way in which this system functions.

In the upper set of waveforms the control signal provides a constant clock frequency, and the normal output waveform is produced. In this example it is a triangular signal. In the lower set of waveforms the initial clock frequency is higher, but it is then decreased to a slower rate than normal so that overall each output cycle lasts the normal time. The result of the variation in clock frequency is to compress the first part of the waveform, and to stretch out the final section (as shown in the bottom waveform).

The 'phase distortion' name is derived from the fact that the phase of the output signal is changed. By speeding up the clock rate, when the signal should be 90 degrees into its cycle it could be (say) 130 degrees into it. The increase in clock rate is always matched by a reduction later in the waveform, so that the 360 degrees point is always reached at the correct time.

Phase envelopes

The amount of phase distortion is controlled by the DCW envelope generator. The Casio envelope generators are sophisticated devices having no less than eight stages, as shown in Fig.3.9. They are set up in a manner which is similar to the Roland LA type, but with rates of rise/fall rather than a certain time per stage. Obviously some very elaborate envelope shapes can be produced, but in most cases there is substantial 'over-kill' available. This does not matter in practice as there is no obligation to use all eight available stages. Three stages are sufficient for a standard ADSR envelope shape, as can be seen from Fig.3.10. The user specifies which phase will act as the sustain one, and which is the final one.

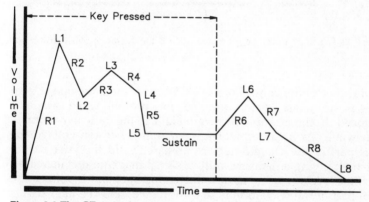

Figure 3.9 The CZ series have sophisticated eight stage envelope shapers

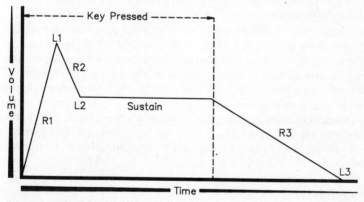

Figure 3.10 For relatively simple envelope shapes only a few of the CZ envelope stages need be used

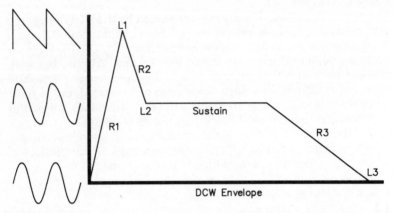

Figure 3.11 The DCW envelope generator controls the degree of phase distortion

Returning to the control of the DCW, with the envelope at zero there is no phase distortion, and the normal wave shape is produced. In the example shown in Fig.3.11 the basic waveform is a sinewave. At an intermediate envelope generator voltage the initial part of the waveform is compressed, and the later part is stretched, giving a distorted output signal that contains increased harmonic levels. At the maximum envelope generator voltage the initial part of the waveform is so compressed, and the later part is so stretched out, that the output waveform is a sawtooth (ramp) type. This produces an output signal that has a very strong harmonic content.

In its effect this system is very much as if the envelope generator was controlling a lowpass filter. The effective filter frequency is quite low, so that there is no harmonic content with the envelope voltage at zero. There is no equivalent to the frequency control of an analogue synthesizer's VCF, but with the multi-stage envelope shaper you can effectively start and finish the DCW at other than zero, effectively raising the filter frequency. A variable keyboard amount can be added to the DCW envelope voltage, and in this respect it is the same as the VCF section of an analogue synthesizer.

PD waveforms
The CZ synthesizers have a basic repertoire of eight waveforms, as detailed in Fig.3.12. Some of these are standard analogue

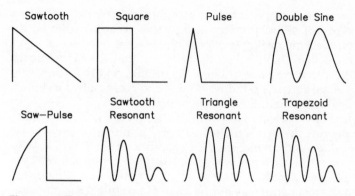

Figure 3.12 The basic PD waveforms

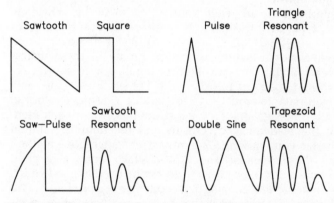

Figure 3.13 The basic waveforms can be joined in pairs to produce more complex waveforms

synthesizer waveforms, but the double sine and resonance types are not. The importance of these becomes apparent when you realize that the DCW provides what is effectively lowpass filtering, but it does not have any equivalent to a resonance control. If a waveform with strong resonance is needed, you have to start with a waveform that has a suitable frequency spectrum.

There is actually an alternative method of obtaining resonance type effects, and this is to use two DCOs. With most twin VCO analogue synthesizers the outputs of the two VCOs are simply mixed and fed into the signal processing chain. With the PD system the two DCOs have separate signal processing circuits, and it is the processed outputs that are mixed (or ring modulated). This gives plenty of scope for producing some complex sounds. By using the 'detune' facility it is possible to have one oscillator set over three octaves higher than the other, so that any harmonic up to the fifteenth can be accentuated. As the second oscillator has its own envelope generator, it does not have to accentuate the chosen harmonic during the full envelope period.

It is possible to select two waveforms from each DCO. This does not simply mix the two signals together, but instead it seems that they are added end-to-end, as in the examples of Fig.3.13. The only restriction on the pairing of waveforms is that two resonance types cannot be used together. To my ears at any rate, the differences between the resonance waveforms seem to be quite small anyway.

Sound programming
The CZ synthesizers are well known for their 'fat' analogue synthesizer type sounds. This is perhaps not surprising as although the methods used are in truth far removed from conventional analogue synthesis, programming of these instruments is very similar. Anyone who is familiar with subtractive synthesis should soon get to grips with PD synthesis. The main difference you have to adjust to is the lack of a resonance control on the pseudo-filter section of these instruments. Some experimentation with the resonance waveforms and the detuning should soon familiarize you with the CZ synthesizer's alternative method of handling these sounds. The CZ1's 'sitar' preset is a good example of how a resonance waveform can be used to good effect. In fact this demonstrates the use of the pitch envelope shaper, two DCOs with separate DCW envelope shapes, and some other facets of PD sound synthesis to very good effect. With any synthesizer it is well worth listening carefully to the preset sounds and studying the parameters used to produce them. The presets are produced by programmers who have built up a lot of experience at programming that particular instrument, and you can learn from their experience in this way.

Some useful effects to try are two DCO signals with one DCW providing decreasing 'filtering' while the other provides increased 'filtering'. A fluctuating envelope shape can produce some dynamic filtering effects, and these can be enhanced having the DCOs with the 'filtering' out-of-phase. Varying the pitch at the beginning of a note is something else that can often be used to good effect. A digital low frequency oscillator (DLFO) is included, but is restricted to pitch modulation. However, as explained above, the DCW envelope can provide a limited but useful form of DCW modulation, and the same system could be applied to the DCA in order to give a form of tremolo. A useful feature of the DLFO is that there is a delay parameter which enables the vibrato to be held off for a period at the beginning of each note. Noise, ring modulation, portamento and the other usual analogue synthesizer gadgets are all included.

Although the CZ synthesizers are often likened to analogue synthesizers, and have clearly been designed to be as compatible as possible with analogue instruments as far as programming is concerned, their capabilities go beyond those of any analogue synthesizer I have used. The CZ1 is a formidable instrument with its built-in chorus effect, 16 note polyphony (8 with twin DCO sounds), 5 octave full-size velocity sensitive keyboard with after-touch, and 8 channel multi-timbral capability. Their multi-timbral capability has made the CZ series very popular with those engaged in MIDI sequencing.

Additive synthesis

All the methods of synthesis described so far have been what could broadly be termed subtractive synthesis. They all involve the use of filters, or some form of pseudo filtering technique. Additive synthesis is a totally different concept which is a sort of inverse of the subtractive technique. Fig.3.14 shows the basic setup used for additive synthesis.

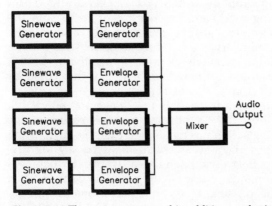

Figure 3.14 The arrangement used in additive synthesis

If all waveforms are made up from sinewave components, it follows that it must be possible to synthesize any waveform using a number of sinewave generators set to the appropriate frequencies. Simply mixing the outputs from a number of sinewave generators is not sufficient for practical synthesis as it only provides a constant waveform. In order to provide changes in timbre during the course of the sound it is necessary to have a separate envelope shaper for each sinewave generator. In Fig.3.14 there are four sinewave generators and envelope shapers, but in a practical system there would ideally be six or more stages.

The potential of a good additive synthesizer is almost limitless, but unfortunately it is a fairly difficult and expensive system to implement well and, as yet, it has not achieved great popularity. If you know the harmonic structure of a sound there is obviously little difficulty in setting up the sinewave generators to give the appropriate type of signal. Rather than setting the absolute frequencies of the sinewave generators, normally one generator is used to provide the fundamental and the frequencies of the others are specified in the form of ratios. Thus, for the second, third and fifth harmonics, ratios of two, three and five would be specified.

For optimum versatility it should be possible to specify fractional ratios so that non-harmonically related frequencies can be obtained. This effectively enables ring modulation to be obtained without actually using any ring modulation. Where additive synthesis is at its weakest is with signals that call for very large numbers of component frequencies. There will then be an inadequate number of sinewave generators available. Even if an instrument with dozens of sinewave sources was produced, setting everything up properly would take an eternity. A better way of producing ring modulation effects might be to split the sinewave generators into two groups, and then ring modulate the two output signals. Similarly, generating a noise signal using additive synthesis would definitely be doing things the hard way. It is more practical to have a filtered noise source that could be mixed into the output from the sinewave generators.

With additive synthesis it is possible to achieve any effect that is obtainable with subtractive synthesis, but this relies on the envelope shapers being suitably versatile. For example, by putting peaks in the envelopes and having them staggered slightly it is possible to obtain an effect very much like a swept filter having a medium to high resonance setting. With a double peak in each envelope it would be possible to obtain dual resonance effects. Provided there are enough sinewave generators and the envelope

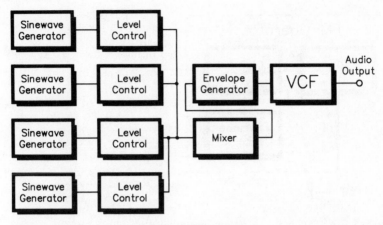

Figure 3.15 A simplified method of additive synthesis

generators are suitably refined, this is an extremely versatile method of sound synthesis. It can provide sounds that are beyond the capabilities of conventional analogue instruments, and in theory can generate any sound whatever.

It is possible to have a watered down system of additive synthesis, as outlined in Fig.3.15. This has sinewave generators, but each one is equipped with a simple level control instead of an envelope shaper. This only gives a fixed output waveform, but a VCF is used to provide changes in timbre during the course of the envelope. This system is as much subtractive synthesis as it is additive synthesis ('suditive' synthesis?).

FM synthesis

Casio's PD synthesizers have dominated the low cost synthesizer market for some years, and Yamaha's frequency modulation (FM) synthesis has been equally dominant at the other end of the market. In fact there are now some low cost FM synthesizers and expanders available, although these are somewhat simplified versions of the higher cost FM synthesizers.

Operators and algorithms
Two terms you cannot avoid if you become involved with FM synthesis are 'operator' and 'algorithm'. An FM operator is a basic sound generating unit, and in a typical FM synthesizer (such as

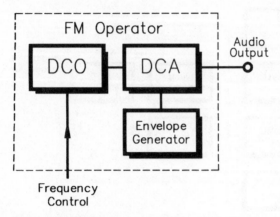

Figure 3.16 An FM operator is a fairly simple device

the legendary Yamaha DX7) there are six of these operators. An operator is a fairly simple device by modern technological standards, and it uses the arrangement shown in Fig.3.16. The DCO is a sinewave type, and the frequency control input is not just used to control the pitch of the oscillator from the keyboard. It is also used as a modulation input that can be fed from other operators. The DCA and envelope generator act as a conventional envelope shaper, which is usually a five phase type (including the sustain phase).

A useful feature of the envelope generators of FM synthesizers is their keyboard rate mode. This gives rates of change that become progressively slower as lower pitched notes are played. This gives longer envelope times on lower notes, like acoustic instruments such as pianos and harps. The FM synthesizer envelope shapers are much like those fitted to LA synthesizers, but with one less phase. They are perhaps more like the Casio envelope generators, as it is the rate of change from one level to another that the programmer specifies, and not a time for each phase. An unusual feature of the FM envelope generators is a mode that gives increasing or decreasing envelope levels either side of a specified note. There is no obvious acoustic instrument parallel to this, but it can produce some interesting and useful effects.

An algorithm is merely a method of connecting two or more operators together. Parallel connection of operators means simply mixing their audio outputs together and ignoring the frequency

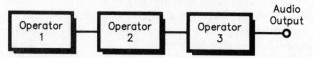

Figure 3.17 FM operators in the series method of connection

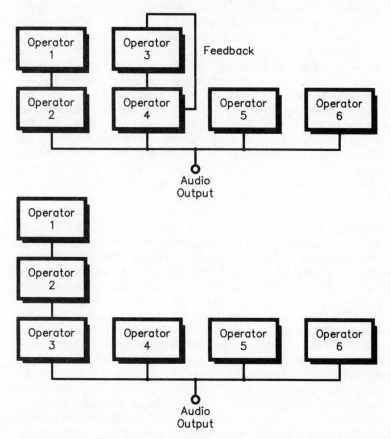

Figure 3.18 Two six-operator FM algorithms

control inputs. This gives a setup that provides what is really conventional additive synthesis. The alternative method of connection is series linking where the audio output of one operator is connected to the frequency control input of the next, as in Fig.3.17. You are not restricted to using one method of connection or the other. It is quite acceptable (and normal) to use a combination of the two methods. With six operators available this gives a number of possible algorithms (typically thirty two). Fig.3.18 shows a couple of example six operator algorithms.

It is easy enough to mentally judge the effect of parallel connected operators, but series connection is a much more difficult proposition. A complex series/parallel setup is even more difficult to contend with. FM synthesizers are not noted for being particularly easy to program, and are famed more for their impressive range of sounds. Whereas familiarity with conventional analogue synthesis is a decided asset when programming many modern synthesizers, with FM synthesis it may prove to be a hindrance. These two methods of sound synthesis lack any obvious common ground. If you try looking for parallels between analogue and FM synthesis, and attempt to adjust an FM instrument as if it was an analogue type, you will probably get nowhere fast. However, as we shall see later, some rough analogies can prove helpful when initially undertaking FM programming, provided they are not taken too far.

Sidebands
In order to program an FM synthesizer effectively you need to understand what happens when one operator modulates another. Vibrato is a form of frequency modulation, but the modulating signal is at a sub-audio frequency, and the modulated tone can be heard to vary in pitch. With FM synthesis the modulating signal is normally at an audio frequency, and the varying in pitch of the modulated tone cannot be heard as such. The effect of this form of modulation is really more like ring modulation, with new frequencies being generated. Like ring modulation, the new frequencies are not necessarily harmonically related to either of the input frequencies.

The in-depth mathematics of FM synthesis are quite involved, and for most users are not worth the effort involved in mastering them. The basics of the FM mathematics are much more simple, and the effect of frequency modulation is to generate 'sidebands'. This is similar to ring modulation, with sum and difference frequencies being produced. For instance, with a 100Hz signal modulating a 1kHz (1000Hz) signal, the new frequencies produced are at 1.1kHz (1kHz + 100Hz = 1.1kHz) and 900Hz (1kHz − 100Hz = 900Hz). These are respectively the upper and lower sidebands. In FM synthesis terminology an operator that acts as a modulation source is (logically) called a 'modulator' (or sometimes a 'controller'), and one that provides part of the audio output signal is called a 'carrier'.

Frequency modulation differs from ring modulation in that with frequency modulation the carrier frequency does appear in the output signal. The carrier is reduced by the application of frequency modulation, and the greater the modulation depth, the larger the reduction in the carrier frequency. Also, with suitably strong modulation, further sideband products are generated. These are spaced above and below the carrier frequency by an amount equal to a multiple of the modulation frequency. In our previous example the modulation frequency was 100Hz, and the new frequencies would therefore be at multiples of 100Hz above and below the 1kHz carrier frequency. In other words, there would be new products at 1.1kHz, 1.2kHz, 1.3kHz, etc., and 900Hz, 800Hz, 700Hz, etc. With strong enough modulation you would theoretically end up with negative frequencies. Unless you can get time to run backwards you cannot have a negative frequency! Apparently what you actually get is a positive frequency, but 180 degrees out of phase with the positive frequencies.

This clearly raises the possibility of generating some quite complex signals. Even with just one heavily modulated carrier a fairly complex output signal can be produced. The signal can be made even more complex by using more carriers (with or without modulation) and (or) modulating a modulator. A further complication is that an operator does not have to have its pitch controlled by the keyboard. With all the operators having their pitches controlled from the keyboard the character of the sound does not change from one note to another. Any apparent change in the timbre is due to the way human hearing perceives sound, and the limitations of its frequency response. With one or more of the operators disconnected from the keyboard the sound will probably change quite drastically from one note to the next.

Feedback
You will notice that in one of the algorithms shown in Fig.3.18 there is a 'feedback' connection which takes some of the output from one operator and feeds it back to the input of an earlier one. The feedback amount is normally variable, and its effect is to increase the strengths of the sideband components. Taken to excess it gives a sort of noise signal.

FM sounds

There are no VCFs or DCFs to control the 'colour' of the sound, but remember that with FM synthesis each operator has its own envelope shaper. This gives control over the strength of each carrier frequency (plus any modulation frequencies it carries) during the course of the overall envelope, as well as permitting the degree of modulation on each carrier to be varied. The programmer has tremendous control over the sound of the instrument, and an enormous repertoire of sounds available. Unfortunately, with the more complex algorithms, changing one parameter can have a knock-on effect which has a drastic effect on the sound. Also, FM synthesis is a relatively complex business anyway, which makes it hard to predict what a particular algorithm and set of parameters will sound like. The effects of changes to parameters can be equally difficult to forecast. Some users quickly master FM synthesis, but others find it more difficult to deal with.

Getting started with FM programming

The easy way to start is to use all the operators as carriers, and to use additive synthesis. With six oscillators available there is reasonable scope for producing good sounds with this method. By using odd and even harmonics (pulse and sawtooth waveforms) some string and brass type sounds can be produced, or with odd numbered harmonics only (triangle and square waveforms) wood-wind and other sounds can be produced. The exact wave shape and brightness of the sound are controlled by the relative amplitudes of the component frequencies, and the envelopes are used to control the changes in timbre. For most acoustic instrument sounds the harmonics must be made to die away to zero faster than the fundamental. The higher the harmonic, the more rapidly it should decay. Of course, you do not have to synthesize an acoustic instrument, and the harmonics can be shaped in any way you wish. FM synthesizers give plenty of scope for producing original and impressionistic sounds.

Do not overlook the fact that an operator can be used as a modulator at a fixed sub-audio frequency in order to provide vibrato. You then have the luxury of an envelope generator for the LFO. On the face of it there is a restriction of one waveform as an operator can only generate sinewave signals. However, the modulator could be modulated by a modulator in order to produce a more complex vibrato effect, although this does not leave many operators for other purposes.

There is an LFO available which can be used for both pitch and amplitude modulation of operators (i.e. it can provide both vibrato and tremolo). Pitch modulation depth is the same for all operators, but the amplitude modulation depth is individually adjustable. Using the LFO for modulation purposes brings the advantage of having several waveforms available, and it leaves all the operators available for other purposes.

FM/analogue analogies

Using an FM instrument as an additive synthesizer is a relatively easy way to get started, but it is largely under-utilizing the capabilities of the instrument. There are loose analogies between some FM controls and those on analogue synthesizers. These really are only loose analogies, but they might be helpful when first getting underway with true FM synthesis. They can help you to develop a proper system for setting up required sounds, instead of just adjusting controls at random in the hope of obtaining the desired result.

The ratio of the carrier frequency to the modulator frequency determines the wave shape. You do not normally need to bother about the actual frequencies involved – it is the ratio of one frequency to the other that tells you what harmonics will be produced or, where appropriate, what non-harmonic products will be generated.

In the most simple example (part 1 of Fig.3.19) the modulator and carrier have the same frequency. With a 1 to 1 ratio all harmonics are generated, giving the types of sound that would be generated by an analogue synthesizer using a sawtooth waveform. A 2 to 1 modulator/carrier ratio generates only the odd numbered harmonics. This must be so, because the sidebands are spaced from the carrier by an amount equal to the modulation frequency. In this case the modulation frequency is the second harmonic of the carrier frequency, and sidebands are generated at the third harmonic, fifth harmonic, seventh harmonic, etc. It might at first seem that the even numbered harmonics would be produced, but you have to bear in mind that the new frequencies are centred on the carrier frequency, which effectively boosts them by one harmonic. Remember that the first sideband above the carrier is at a frequency which is equal to the sum of the carrier and modulator frequencies, which will obviously be three times the carrier frequency. This produces a square type waveform that can be used to produce the usual squarewave type sounds. A modulator to carrier ratio of 3 to 1 generates only every third harmonic, starting with the fourth. This gives a 'fat' pulse type sound.

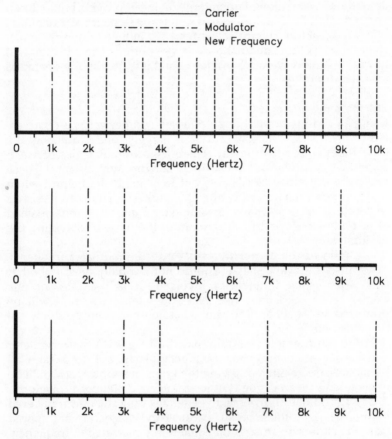

Figure 3.19 Some examples of harmonic products generated by frequency modulation

Choosing ratios that give a lot of non-harmonic components gives an effect that is the FM equivalent of an analogue synthesizer's ring modulation.

The number of harmonics generated (or other new frequencies) and their strength depends on the depth of modulation. The deeper the modulation, the stronger the new frequencies and the greater the number that are produced. The envelope generator of the modulator therefore provides a function that is broadly similar to the envelope shaper of the VCF in an analogue synthesizer. The envelope shaper of the carrier controls the envelope of the overall output signal, and is equivalent to the envelope generator controlling the VCA of an analogue synth. Additional operators can be used as carriers to boost certain harmonics, and with staggered peaks in their envelopes an equivalent to the resonance of an analogue synthesizer's VCF can be achieved.

These analogies can be useful when getting started with programming FM synthesizers, but are of no more than limited help. There is no substitute for 'hands-on' experience, and a lot of adjusting control settings and listening carefully to the results is the only way to master any synthesizer. Practical experience is especially important with the more complex algorithms that use multiple modulation, as these defy easy description and explanation. It is important to choose an algorithm that is suitable for the type of sound you are trying to produce. For simple sounds there may be no need to use FM synthesis at all, and additive synthesis with all the operators used as carriers will probably suffice. For more complex sounds such as bells, saxophones, and guitars a more complex algorithm using one or more modulators will be required.

4-operator FM synths

We have been talking here in terms of six operator instruments, but some low cost FM synthesizers only have four. These offer little scope for additive synthesis, and modulation is needed for many comparatively simple sounds. In some cases the operators have been designed to produce waveforms other than sinewaves in an attempt to compensate for the missing operators. This can certainly enrich the available sounds, but does not make programming any easier.

Programmers

A common grumble about modern synthesizers is the difficulty involved in setting up a complete set of parameters. This seems to involve a lot of tedious button pushing rather than twiddling of analogue synthesizer style control knobs. Looking at the two synthesizers and two samplers in my system there are only two control knobs in evidence, and one of these is merely a master volume control! Altering control settings is normally a matter of entering the number allocated to the desired control via a keypad, and then using two push buttons to increment/decrement the control's setting, as indicated on an LCD or LED display. Once you get used to using an instrument it is possible to enter data reasonably fast, but this system is used for its compactness and low cost rather than its speed and convenience.

Plug-in control boxes (programmers) are available for some synthesizers, and these have a number of control knobs that represent a much quicker and more convenient means of adjusting the instrument's settings. These are often quite expensive, but will probably be worth the money for someone who intends to do a substantial amount of programming. Unfortunately, most of these programmers are only suitable for one instrument, or perhaps for two or three very similar instruments. If you have several synthesizers of different types you may well need a separate control unit for each one.

Many electronic music systems are computer based these days, and a computer plus suitable software offers another means of adjusting some instruments. Again, this can be a very much faster and more convenient way of doing things. Usually there are a number of on-screen controls which are manipulated via the computer's mouse, and control settings are sent to the synthesizer via a MIDI link. Provided you already have a suitable computer, this method can offer a comparatively low cost solution to the problem. With a few synthesizer modules, this represents the only way of gaining access to all the parameters of the sound generator circuits!

4 Sound samplers

It is debatable whether or not a sound sampler can be legitimately called a type of synthesizer. After all, samplers simply record a sound and play it back again. They are not synthesizing sound in the normally accepted sense. On the other hand, most samplers are not limited to simply recording sounds and playing them back in their original form. They are usually capable of providing some sort of signal processing or manipulation. A further point worth noting is that many samplers do have some true synthesis capability, and are not restricted to recording real sounds. In fact a sound sampler, particularly with the aid of a computer, can have considerable sound synthesis capability.

Whether or not sound samplers can be legitimately regarded as a form of synthesizer, no apologies are made for considering the subject in some detail in this book. They are used side by side with synthesizers and in broadly the same way as synthesizers. They are very much a part of the synthesizer world, and seem to be playing an ever more important role in electronic music. If your primary interest is in acoustic instruments sounds, then sound samplers are probably better suited to your needs than any synthesizers. It would be a mistake to overlook their potential at generating weird and wonderful electronic sounds though.

Analogue-digital/digital-analogue

In the previous chapter we briefly covered the subject of DCOs and wavetables, and sound sampling is an extension of this idea. Instead of mathematically calculating the values required for the required waveform and programming them into the ROM chip, real sounds are recorded in the memory chip by 'digitizing' them. This involves sampling the input voltage from the microphone at regular intervals, and converting these voltages into corresponding values that are stored in the memory circuit. As the 'read only' part of its name implies, ROM can not be used for this type of thing. It can only be programmed at the manufacturing stage. ROM is used as the method of sample storage in some instruments, but these are types that have a number of preset sounds, and usually have no facility for the user to produce any do-it-yourself samples. These are mostly drum machines which can play only the samples supplied on ROM with the machine, or possibly those available on some form of plug-in ROM cartridge.

The type of memory used in samplers is RAM (random access memory). This title is not a particularly meaningful one, as ROM and every other type of memory chip I have ever encountered have had this random access capability (i.e. any value in the chip can be read whenever desired — they do not have to be accessed in any particular order). The main point about RAM is that it can store data written to it by other devices in the circuit, and it is not programmed at all at the manufacturing stage. As this type of memory circuit suffers complete amnesia as soon as the power is switched off, programming during the manufacturing process is not a practical proposition anyway.

Sampler basics

Fig.4.1 shows the basic arrangement used in a sampler, albeit in a greatly over-simplified form. The microphone converts the

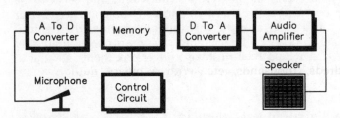

Figure 4.1 Highly simplified representation of a sound sampling system

received sound waves into corresponding electrical signals, and these are fed to the analogue to digital (A to D) converter. This converts the analogue input signal into some form of digital representation that is stored in memory. The control circuit determines how often new samples are taken and stored in the memory circuit. The number of samples that can be stored in memory varies from one sampler to another. Memory capacity is normally quoted in kilobytes, or kilowords. A byte is eight bits of binary data. There is no need to delve deeply into the binary numbering system in order to understand the basics of sound samplers, but a few fundamentals are a definite help in mastering some of the main terminology of samplers.

1s and 0s

Digital circuits do not deal in varying voltage levels, such as the signal obtained from a microphone. They only recognise and provide two signal levels called logic 0 and logic 1 (also known as 'low' and 'high' respectively). Logic 0 is represented by a very low voltage of only about 1 volt or less, while logic 1 is represented by a higher (but still quite modest) voltage of about 4 to 5 volts. One logic output cannot accurately represent the voltage from a microphone, or any other analogue value. It can only count from 0 to 1 with no fractions or decimals allowed!

While one digital output may be of limited value, a number of them used together can represent any required number with good accuracy. Usually digital lines are used in a block of eight, or multiples of eight. Eight bits are called a 'byte', and 16 bits are usually termed a 'word'. This second term is less rigidly defined though, and other numbers of digital bits are sometimes referred to as words. Using eight bits you can have numbers such as 11110000, but on the face of it this is not much more use than a single output. Using the normal decimal numbering system, digital signals are totally useless. However, using the binary numbering system they suddenly become very much more useful.

If you are not familiar with the binary numbering system, the basics are not really too difficult to grasp. With decimal numbers the columns represent (from right to left) the number of units, tens, hundreds, thousands, etc. With a binary number they represent the units, twos, fours, eights, sixteens, thirty twos, and so on. The binary number 1101 therefore breaks down as one unit, no twos, one four, and one eight (reading 1101 from right to left). In other words it is equivalent to thirteen $(1 + 4 + 8 = 13)$ in the normal decimal numbering system.

With the eight bits of a byte any integer (whole number) from 0 to 255 can be represented. When applied to a sound sampler, this means that each input voltage sample is converted to one of 256 different digital values. An eight bit system can give reasonable audio quality, but it provides far from hi-fi standards of reproduction. Most sound samplers use 12 or 16 bit circuits. These respectively provide 4096 and 65536 different sample values, and a far higher standard of performance. They require more memory though, since each sample will not fit into an 8 bit byte of memory.

If the memory of an 8 bit sampler is given as 32k, it can therefore store 32000 samples (or 32678 to be precise, as 1k is 1024 and not 1000 bytes). Where the memory capacity of a sampler is given in words, the word length will normally be equal to the number of bits used for each sample. A memory capacity of 32k words would therefore permit the storage of 32678 samples whether the sampler is a 16 or 12 bit type. If the memory capacity of a 16 bit sampler is specified in bytes, remember that two bytes per sample are required. 32k bytes will therefore store only 16384 16 bit samples.

Returning to our simplified sampler, once a full set of samples have been stored, the unit can be switched to the playback mode. The A to D converter is then disconnected from the memory circuit, and the digital to analogue (D to A) converter is connected in its place. Samples can then be read from memory by the D to A converter, and converted back to a series of voltages. These are amplified and fed to a loudspeaker which converts the electrical signals back into sound waves. During playback the system is functioning very much like a DCO. An important difference is that a DCO usually only has a single cycle stored in memory. A sound sampler would typically have a few hundred cycles per sample, and possibly as many as several thousand.

Sample quality

Fig.4.2 helps to clarify the way in which the digitizing and playback process operates. In this example the samples are taken at 0.1 millisecond (0.0001 second) intervals, which is a rate of 10000 per second. Each time a sample is taken the converter stores the corresponding value in RAM. Due to the finite resolution of the converter it must effectively do a certain amount of rounding up and rounding down as it cannot provide a precise value for each input voltage. For instance, with a converter that increments in 0.1 volt steps, an input voltage of 2.369 volts would be converted to a value of 23 or (more probably) 24. During playback the D to A converter outputs a series of voltages that, more or less, recreate the original waveform.

There are errors in that the output voltages used are the nearest ones the resolution of the system permits, and are not exactly the same as the original input voltages at the times the samples were taken. In our earlier example an input of 2.369 volts was converted to a value of 23 or 24. At the D to A converter this would be converted to 2.3 or 2.4 volts. Either way there is obviously a small

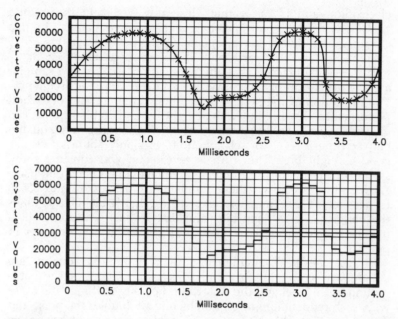

Figure 4.2 The audio digitizing process. Digital audio generally sounds better than it looks!

error. Also, each output voltage is maintained for 0.1 milliseconds, giving a stepped output waveform and not the continuously varying input waveform.

Samplers have a lowpass filter at the output, and this to some extent smooths out the steps in the waveform. This filtering only removes high frequency components on the output signal though, and it is needed to prevent these signals from having an adverse effect on any equipment fed from the output of the unit. It will not remove any audio frequency components put onto the output signal by this stepping.

You will notice that in Fig.4.2 the converter values are all positive, even though the input voltages will be a mixture of positive and negative values. A bias circuit ahead of the A to D converter is used to raise all the input voltages by an amount that is just sufficient to ensure that they are always positive. Another circuit at the D to A converter effectively reduces all the output voltages by a similar amount so that a dual polarity output signal, like the input signal, is produced. This requires some very simple electronics, and is easier than designing a system that would genuinely deal in both positive and negative values. In this example the notional converter is a 16 bit type having a 0 to 65535 value range, and the bias level is therefore set at about 32678.

The two main factors that affect the output quality of a sampler are the resolution of the converters and the sampling frequency. The resolution of the system determines the noise and distortion performance. Talking in terms of eight, 12 and 16 bit systems can give the impression that there is not much difference in the quality between these levels of resolution. 16 bits only sounds twice as good as eight bits. The truth is revealed if you consider these systems in terms of the number of voltage levels each one uses. As we saw previously, these numbers are 256, 4096, and 65536 respectively. These figures would suggest that 12 bits give 16 times the performance of eight bits, and that 16 bit resolution gives a further 16 fold increase in quality. This is the way it operates in practice.

In fact the basic mathematics of digital audio quality are delightfully simple. Each extra bit gives a halving of the background noise level and the distortion. Looking at things the other way, each reduction in resolution by one bit doubles the noise and distortion. A good 16 bit system will achieve a signal to noise ratio of about −96dB, and distortion of only about 0.002%. This is the resolution used for compact discs, and is more than adequate for most purposes. Finding an amplifier and loudspeakers to live up to this level of quality is problematical. With 12 bit resolution the noise and distortion figures are still quite respectable at approximately −72dB and well under 0.1% respectively. This is comparable to a good FM tuner or cassette deck, and is adequate for most purposes. Eight bit resolution gives less impressive results with a signal to noise ratio of about 48dB and distortion approaching 0.5%. This is comparable to a cassette recorder which is not equipped with any form of noise reduction system.

Recording level

These figures give what is not really a totally accurate view of digital audio performance. The signal to noise ratios are accurate enough, but they assume that everything in the system is working to perfection. In practice the digital circuits will achieve marginally less than their theoretical accuracy, and there will usually be some analogue circuits (amplifiers and filters) that will slightly degrade the noise performance. However, performance in this respect is usually quite close to the theoretical maximum performance levels. Distortion performance is a very different proposition. A good practical system will achieve something close to the distortion figures quoted earlier, but only on signals that use the full value range of the converter. It is quite easy to see why this should be if you consider what happens if a signal uses less than the full resolution of the converter. If you have (say) a 12 bit system, but the input signal only uses the middle 10% of its range, the signal will be digitized over a range of values that only covers from around 1850 to 3350 (bearing in mind that 12 bit resolution gives 4096 different values). This is no better than using a nine bit converter covering a range of 0 to 511, but with the full range used. In both cases only nine bit performance is obtained. The lower the input signal level is made, the higher the noise and distortion levels become.

Clipping

In fact it is the relative noise and distortion levels that increase. The absolute noise and distortion levels remain the same regardless of the input level. Both are far less noticeable at higher signal levels as the signal is proportionately much higher and masks them. It is important with samplers, as with any form of recording system, to get the recording level right so that the full dynamic range of the system is utilized. On the other hand, you must avoid having the recording level so high that 'clipping' occurs (Fig.4.3). The effect of clipping is to produce strong harmonic products and intermodulation products (similar to ring modulation), and its effect on the sound is somewhat worse than one might expect from looking at the waveforms of Fig.4.3.

In fact the situation can be worse with some digital audio circuits. Taking the input below zero volts generally results in a reading of 0 being produced from the A to D converter, but taking the input voltage above the full scale value does not always produce a full scale reading. A good many converters cycle right back to zero and then produce a reading equal to the amount by which the input signal has exceeded the full scale voltage. This results in the output voltage during playback going from its peak positive level to its peak negative level as the clipping threshold is exceeded, and then making the reverse journey as the signal drops back through the clipping level. This effect is sometimes called 'digital clipping', and it produces what is just about the worst possible form of distortion. It is something which must be avoided

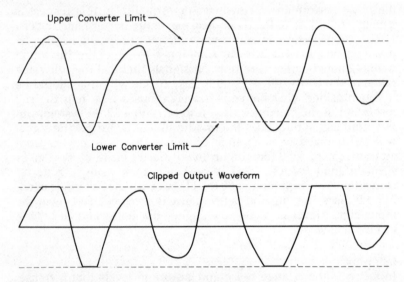

Figure 4.3 Setting the recording level too high results in clipping and severe distortion. It sounds worse than it looks

at all costs. Fortunately, most sound samplers have circuits that by one means or another stop this sort of clipping from occurring.

Companders

For good results you must have a high enough recording level, but this is not a complete solution. Most of the sounds recorded using a sampler start at a high level and then gradually die away to zero. With inadequate resolution the quality of the output signal will be clearly heard to degrade as the sound decays. There are ways of obtaining improved results from digital audio systems. One is to use a 'compander' system. This is a method of noise reduction that is often used in tape recording, and it relies on compressing the signal during record. In other words, as the signal level drops, the recording level is automatically increased. This keeps the recording level reasonably high even on low level signals, and maintains good noise and distortion performance. Obviously it changes the dynamic levels of the played-back signal, but this problem is corrected by an expander. This reduces the gain on low level signals (the lower the signal level the lower its gain), and in theory it restores the signal to its original levels.

In practice there can be problems with compander systems that give more than modest increases in the signal to noise ratio of an audio system. Although this system has its advantages, it does not seem to have gained widespread acceptance in the sampler world. I would have to say that the companded 8 bit systems I have experimented with certainly seemed to compare quite well with standard 12 bit systems.

Another method of improving performance is to use converters that do not have equal increments from one value to the next. The basic idea is to have small increments near the central bias level, with steadily increasing increments out towards the clipping level. While it may seem as though this would introduce a lot of distortion, the lack of linearity in the scaling of the A to D converter will not introduce any distortion provided the D to A converter uses exactly the same scaling. The advantage of this method is that it gives lots of very fine increments on low level signals, and consequently has far lower noise and distortion figures. In electronics (as with everything else in life) you do not normally get something for nothing, and this increased performance on small signals is matched by reduced performance at high signal levels. This is due to the much lower resolution on signal peaks.

Rather than having a level of performance that is very high on strong signals, but falls away rapidly as the signal level is reduced, this system provides more consistent results over a range of signal levels. Performance still reduces to some extent as the input level is decreased. While this system has its advantages, it seems to be little used in modern sound samplers. This could be due to technical difficulties, and using higher resolution linear converters and the extra memory they require might be a more practical method. It could just be that high resolution linear devices are better from the marketing point of view.

Frequency response

In the interests of good audio quality it is important to have a high sampling frequency, but not for the reason one might expect. In order to obtain a reasonably accurate output signal it is clearly necessary to take samples very frequently. Otherwise any fine detail on the waveform will be missed by the digitizing process, and inaccuracies in the output signal will result. Increased resolution in the converters always gives improved audio performance in terms of noise and distortion levels, but increased sampling rate does not necessarily improve performance at all. The sampling frequency does not affect the noise and distortion figures of the system at all. It governs the frequency response of the system.

This is fairly obvious if you give it some thought. With an inadequate sampling frequency any small spikes or dips in the waveform are likely to be missed and will not be reflected in the output signal. Any signals of this type must be very brief, and consequently must contain only high frequency components. A fast sampling rate enables the system to follow rapid changes in the signal caused by high frequency components, and gives good high frequency performance. There is no point in using very high sampling frequencies though, because the audio spectrum ends at about 20kHz. A very high sampling rate merely enables the system to handle frequencies that will probably never be present on the input signal, and which you cannot hear anyway. There is good reason for using the lowest possible sampling frequency. This permits the longest possible sampling time for a given amount of memory.

Aliasing distortion

The result of an inadequate sampling rate is clear from the waveforms of Fig.4.4. This has the same input waveform as our earlier digitizing example in Fig.4.2. However, the sampling rate has been reduced by a factor of ten, and the digitized version now bears very little resemblance to the original waveform. With the sampling rate set very low you end up with what is more of a random voltage generator than a sound sampler. The output signal resembles the clock signal used to control the sampling rate more than it resembles the input signal. It is presumably from this that this type of distortion derives its 'aliasing' name.

For adequate results the sampling frequency must be at least double the maximum input frequency, and should ideally be three or more times this frequency. Note that we are not talking here in terms of fundamental input frequencies. It is the highest input frequency of any type (fundamental or harmonic) that determines the minimum acceptable sampling rate. This dictates that in order to accommodate the full audio spectrum a sampling frequency of at least 40kHz is needed, and ideally the sampling frequency should be 60kHz or more. In reality very few samplers can provide rates of 40000 per second or more. This could give the impression that these instruments will produce severe aliasing distortion

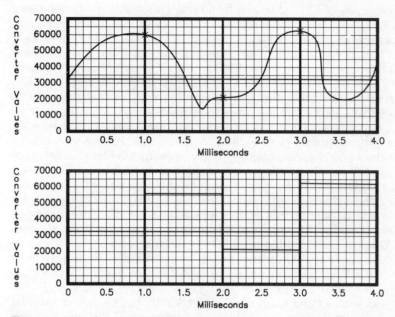

Figure 4.4 An inadequate sampling rate produces aliasing distortion

when fed with an input signal having any high frequency components. In practice this does not happen because sound samplers have lowpass filters at their inputs that prevent any signals having an excessive frequency from reaching the A to D converter. The result of a low sampling rate is therefore a lack of high frequency response on played-back samples rather than any aliasing distortion.

Most samplers will operate at a maximum sampling rate of around 32 to 36kHz. A few offer a maximum of 40 to 50kHz. These instruments that can sample at 40kHz and beyond obviously have the potential of operating with the full audio bandwidth. With sampling frequencies of 32 or 36kHz something less than the full audio bandwidth is provided. In practice a sampling rate of this order can still provide excellent results. It has to be remembered that few people can actually hear a 20kHz signal, and many people cannot hear beyond about 15kHz. Where people can hear these high frequencies, their hearing is still very inefficient over this range. The loss of the top 5kHz of the audio range is less important than you might think. Taking things in context, the frequency responses of FM radios and hi-fi tuners are severely filtered above 15kHz, but few people seem to be aware of this. Only very good cassette recorders and tapes reach the top 5kHz of the audio range. It is not uncommon for samplers to offer quite low sampling frequencies — often below 10kHz. With a sampling rate of around 8 to 10kHz there is clearly a very limited frequency response. The point of providing these low sampling rates is that they enable relatively long sampling times to be used. If you know the amount of memory available and the sampling rate, it is quite easy to work out the sampling period. Simply divide the number of words of memory by the sampling frequency in hertz. Dividing the memory capacity in kilo-words by the frequency in kilohertz will provide an answer that is accurate enough for most purposes (a slight error occurs as there are 1024 words per kilo word, not 1000). A sampler having 32 kilo words of memory and a sampling frequency of 36kHz would therefore provide a sampling time of 0.889 seconds (32 kilo words divided by 36kHz = 0.889 seconds).

A sample frequency that limits the bandwidth of the system to a few kilohertz clearly limits the usefulness of the unit at this rate. Brass sounds and other bright sounds are unlikely to sound very good with a bandwidth of much under 10kHz. Of course, even if a low sample rate results in a somewhat muffled version of the original sound, it might still be quite useful and could have musical possibilities. Some instruments produce very little high frequency output, and will show little or no loss of quality when sampled at relatively low frequencies. Do not jump to the conclusion that a low pitched instrument will always have a very small high frequency content. Some low pitched instruments, such as bowed basses and cellos, have quite strong harmonics well into the upper part of the audio range. A few samplers can operate at very low sampling rates (just a few kilohertz or even less), but the bandwidth is then so limited as to be of little use for sampling and recreating acoustic instrument sounds. Some weird and wonderful bass sounds can be produced though!

Pitch changes

So far we have only considered a sampler when used to record a sound and then play back a perfect replica, or as close to one as the unit can manage anyway. This method offers little scope, and is mainly restricted to percussion sounds. With these the lack of control over the pitch of the instrument and the inability to control the length of reproduced sounds is not usually important. When triggered the unit merely has to reproduce the appropriate burst of sound.

Apart from sampling drum machines, most samplers permit the pitch of a note to be varied over quite wide limits. As a couple of examples, the Akai S700 has a six octave range, while the Ensoniq Mirage has a five octave range. The pitch can be varied by speeding up or slowing down the rate at which samples are outputted during playback. Like changing the speed of a record player or a tape recorder, this gives a proportional change in the pitch of the reproduced sound. A point that should not be overlooked is that it also increases or decreases the duration of the sound. This can be useful for sounds where low pitched notes tend to have longer durations (pianos, harps, etc.), but it might not always give the desired result.

Another method of changing the pitch is to miss out some samples. For example, missing out every other sample raises the pitch of the sound by one octave. As it is not possible to produce additional samples out of thin air, this method can only be used to increase the pitch, and not to reduce it. This method of pitch modification also results in sounds being shortened as they are raised in pitch. For a really wide pitch range a mixture of these methods can be used.

Reducing the playback rate of samples has limited scope for reducing the pitch. It reduces the bandwidth of the reproduced signal and could result in unwanted audio products being generated and clearly heard on the output of the unit. Good filtering will remove any unwanted frequencies that are produced, but there is no easy solution to the decreased bandwidth. Some samplers do seem to use tricks such as variations on the so-called 'over-sampling' technique that was originally developed for use in compact disc players. This factor still remains one of the biggest weaknesses of most samplers.

An important point to bear in mind when producing your own sound samples is that the full pitch range of the instrument is generally only available if the sound is sampled over a very restricted range of notes, or possibly if it is sampled at one particular note. If you sample a bass sound it may not be possible to play it at the top end of the keyboard. Normally you have to tell the sampler the pitch of the sound you are sampling. If you make a mistake here, the notes you play and the ones the instrument will produce will not be the same. If a mistake is made, it may well be possible to adjust the instrument to correct the offset in pitch.

Pitch problems

When undertaking sound sampling there can be some surprising results. A common problem is when a sound is sampled, and is totally transformed when it is played back shifted up or down by more than an octave from its original pitch. In fact most sounds are changed quite drastically if they are transposed by more than an octave. Some sounds are altered quite significantly if they are shifted up or down by even just a few semitones. The human voice is a sound which is often prone to this effect, particularly female voices.

There are a number of reasons for this problem, which tends to seriously complicate the business of sound sampling. One is simply that a reduction in pitch is usually accompanied by a reduction in the bandwidth of the output signal. With an acoustic instrument a reduction in its pitch is usually accompanied by some reduction in the high frequency harmonics, but they are unlikely to be totally eliminated. Designing a system to have a considerably higher upper frequency response limit than the 20kHz maximum of the audio range might improve matters, but in practice this is not an option that is available. Unless the sampled signal contained signals beyond the upper limit of the audio range it would not help anyway.

Another reason for this problem is that the sound produced by most instruments changes slightly from one note to the next, and a cumulative effect gives quite large changes from one octave to the next. Probably the basic sound from the resonator (string, reed or whatever) does not change a great deal over a range of a few octaves, but the effect of the rest of the instrument must be taken into account. Most instruments have some form of hollow body that effectively amplifies the sound of the instrument, but also colours it by accentuating some frequencies more than others. When the pitch of the instrument is altered, the frequencies that are boosted remain the same. This contrasts with a sound sampler, where the accentuated frequencies change in sympathy with the change in pitch of the sound. As a simple example, consider an instrument that has a boosted fourth harmonic with a fundamental pitch of 500Hz. The boosted harmonic is therefore at 2kHz. Raising the pitch of the instrument by an octave takes the fundamental to

1kHz, and the fourth harmonic to 4kHz. Obviously the fourth harmonic is no longer accentuated, and it will be the second harmonic that is boosted (if it is present). Reducing the pitch of the instrument by one octave from its original level has a similar effect. It will be the eighth harmonic and not the fourth one that will be accentuated.

With a sound sampler, if the fourth harmonic is accentuated on the signal that is recorded, then this harmonic will be equally strong at whatever pitch the instrument is played back.

Dynamic problems

In common with most other modern electronic instruments, touch sensitivity seems to be more or less a standard feature for sound samplers. While this is an extremely valuable feature, it is not a complete solution to the dynamics of sampled sounds. Play the keyboard hard and the sound is loud — play gently and the sound is quiet. It is still exactly the same sound though. The sound of an acoustic instrument often changes quite noticeably when it is played harder. In general the sound becomes brighter the harder the instrument is played. There can be other changes in the sound though.

One way of tackling this problem is to sample a sound with the sampled instrument played loudly, and to use a VCF controlled by the keyboard's velocity sensing circuit and an envelope shaper to reduce the brightness of the sound when the keyboard is played gently. Most sound samplers include a VCF, but the sophistication of this part of the instrument, and the circuit that controls it, varies considerably from one instrument to another. In most cases you have what is effectively a conventional analogue synthesizer with the sound sampling circuits used instead of a VCO. In some cases you even have an arrangement that is analogous to a twin VCO synthesizer (as in the Ensoniq Mirage for instance), so that simple chorus type effects and other twin VCO tricks can be performed.

Filtering can also help with the problems caused by pitch changing that were explained previously. However, there is only limited scope for improving the sounds using filtering.

Multi-sampling

Multi-sampling is a feature that is now available on a good many samplers, but it is one of those terms that is not as rigidly defined as it could be. Presumably any sampler that can store more than one sample at a time could be accurately termed a multi-sampler. In some cases the multi-sampling is used to endow the instrument with multi-timbral capability. With a 16 channel multi-timbral sampler you could (almost literally) have an orchestra in a box!

Most multi-samplers have some multi-timbral capability, but they often have the ability to use the multi-sampling in more subtle but equally useful ways. One of these ways is to use the keyboard split mode of operation. This basic method of split operation is not restricted to samplers, and a lot of synthesizers have a similar feature. The general idea is to have one sound assigned to the lower half of the keyboard, and another one assigned to the upper half. Some split keyboard systems are pretty basic, while others are quite sophisticated. The split point might be fixed, or it might be user definable. There might even be the option of more than one user definable split point so that the keyboard can be divided into three or four zones.

One application of this split operation is for a standard form of multi-timbral operation. You have two totally different instrument sounds, and play one with each hand. For sampling there is an interesting alternative. This is to have the same instrument sound in both sections of the keyboard, but to have two different samples. A sample taken at a low pitch for the bottom half of the keyboard, and a sample taken at a higher pitch for the upper half. It may even be possible to have more than two keyboard zones. Ideally there would be one sample per note, and with really awkward sounds even a three or four way split is unlikely to produce very convincing results. Split operation is vastly superior to using one sample right across the keyboard though, and it is good enough for most types of sound. Apart from the complexity involved in having one sample per note, it is impracticable for general use as it requires far too much memory.

An alternative use of multi-sampling is to use a different sample depending on how hard a key is struck. The idea of this is to have two samples of an instrument, one with it played loudly and one with it played softly. Which of these samples is used depends on the key pressure used. Gentle playing automatically selects the soft sample, and hard playing selects the loud sample. Once again, this system is not restricted to a two way split, and it is quite feasible to have several samples and a multi-way velocity split. With many types of sound this can provide much more realistic results.

These two types of split operation are not mutually exclusive, and it is possible to use them together. This system is used to very good effect in some Yamaha pianos which use around twenty samples for one piano sound. However, while this dual multi-way split operation might be very desirable, few (if any) samplers can provide it. The problem is not merely one of the complexities of controlling everything properly and getting the system to function properly. This is clearly quite possible, as it is achieved in the sampling electronic pianos. The main problem is that many samplers do not have sufficient memory to hold all the samples that would be required. The prices of RAM chips have been a bit erratic in recent times, but overall the trend has been downwards, and the amount of memory fitted to samplers seems to be steadily increasing. Some now have one or two megabytes as standard with the option of adding more memory via plug-in cards. Sophisticated multi-sampling is gradually becoming a more practical proposition, but these top flight samplers are still far from cheap.

Loop the loop

A fundamental problem of sound sampling is controlling the length of a sample when it is played back. The correct rhythm is an essential part of any music, and is something that cannot be achieved if a sample is simply played back in full. The duration of notes must be controlled from the keyboard. The ideal way of doing things would be to sample a sound for a very long time, and then use the keyboard to switch the sound on and then switch it off again when the key is released. In practice it is not usually possible to obtain long samples. Even if a sound has a suitably long duration, there will probably be inadequate memory to accommodate it.

The standard way around the problem is to loop the sample. This simply means playing all or most of the sound sample, and then jumping forwards to a certain point and repeating this end part of the sample over and over again. Thus, instead of coming to an abrupt end, the signal is sustained indefinitely. Fig.4.5 shows how a looped signal is normally controlled in practice. The initial attack part of the envelope is the natural shape of the sampled sound. When the end part of the sample is looped, the amplitude of the output signal remains constant. When the key is released the looped signal is still used, but the output level is gradually decreased by a VCA and very simple envelope generator circuit. The envelope generator controls the release time, and this must obviously be set at a sensible release time for the instrument sound in use. For something like a piano a fairly long decay would be

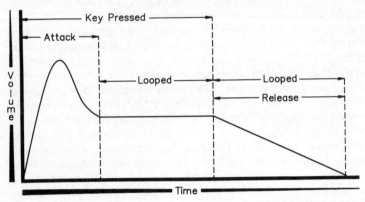

Figure 4.5 The standard method of controlling the envelope of a looped sample

needed, but a woodwind instrument would require a much faster release.

Looping a sample in order to sustain it indefinitely sounds easy enough, but it is usually quite difficult to obtain really good results in practice. The human ear is very exacting and can detect the smallest of imperfections in a sound. A looped sample that looks perfectly all right when its waveform is displayed on an oscilloscope can actually sound absolutely dreadful. Ideally a loop should be as in Fig.4.6, where there is no jump in signal level at the loopback points. This gives a nice regular and click-free output waveform. The basic idea is to loop the signal in such a way that there is no sudden jump in signal level from the end of one loop to the beginning of the next.

This is not achieved in the example shown in Fig.4.7, which would give strong clicks on the output signal and would be totally unusable. This is not the only problem, and comparing Fig.4.6 with Fig.4.7 it should be obvious that the rather poor looping in the second example has resulted in the pitch of the signal being substantially boosted. In order to obtain satisfactory results the looped part of the signal must be a complete cycle, or a number of cycles. In the looped waveform of Fig.4.8 there is no sudden jump in the signal level as the signal goes from the end to the beginning of the loop. The signal is looped over one and a half cycles though, and even with no looping glitches, this would totally alter the character of the sound.

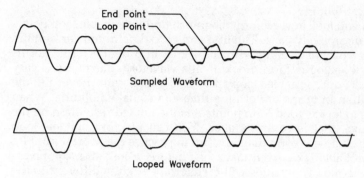

Figure 4.6 A well looped sample that should be free of looping clicks

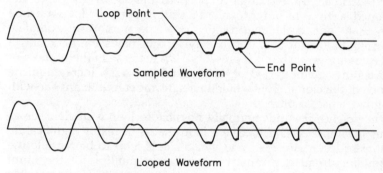

Figure 4.7 This inept looping would produce unusable results

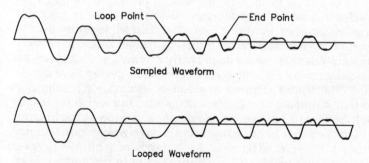

Figure 4.8 This loop has no sudden jump in level but is unusable

Practical looping
When you look at waveform diagrams, finding suitable loop points
looks deceptively easy. The first and crucial point to bear in mind
is that you are dealing with the signal in a digital form, not its
original analogue form. Looking at a waveform diagram it is easy
to pick out suitable loop points because you have infinite
resolution in terms of both the time and signal amplitude. When
trying to locate good loop points it is the limited resolution on the
time axis that is of importance. You can pick out suitable loop
points on a waveform diagram, but in practice the nearest samples
will probably have been taken just before or just after the points
you selected. The values will therefore be slightly different to the
ones you would expect, and the result is likely to be a sizeable
jump in value that will produce a click.

Sometimes a perfectly glitchless loop is unusable because it is
accompanied by a change in pitch as the signal goes into the
looped section. In order to avoid a shift in pitch the loop must be
precisely one cycle in duration, or some number of complete
cycles. If a loop is only 0.98 of a cycle, this may seem to be only a
very minor error, but it represents a 2% increase in the number of
cycles in a given period of time, and hence a 2% increase in the
pitch of the signal. This would be readily apparent to anyone with
a good sense of pitch.

In practice it is not normally possible to loop a single cycle as
this is almost certain to give a loop that is in reality significantly
more or less than one cycle. For a single loop to be feasible the
sampling frequency must be some exact multiple of the input
frequency, or something very close to it. It is not usually possible
to arrange things in this convenient way. By looping over a
number of cycles any shift in pitch can be greatly reduced. A loop
over 0.98 of a cycle gives a 2% increase in pitch, but looping over
9.98 cycles instead of 10 cycles only gives a 0.2% rise in pitch.

There is another consideration that makes looping over a
number of cycles preferable. Most instruments produce very
complex sounds that cannot be properly captured in a single cycle,
and in some cases it could require dozens of cycles to really do
justice to the sound. The usual result of using a short loop is a
sound that is initially very lively and realistic, but which turns into
a simple buzzing sound of inaccurate pitch as soon as the looping
starts! On the other hand, using an excessively long loop will not
be satisfactory either. The most likely problem with a very long
loop is that there will be a significant change in the amplitude of
the signal from the start to the end of the loop. This makes it hard

(and probably impossible) to obtain a really smooth transition from the end to the beginning of the loop. Even if smooth looping can be achieved, the changes in the amplitude of the signal give a sort of tremolo effect.

Auto looping

Modern samplers almost invariably have some form of automatic looping. This may seem like the sort of application to which a microprocessor is well suited, but any form of pattern matching is something that seems to stretch the capabilities of any microprocessor. Most automatic looping will give a loop of good pitch and free from any serious glitching, but microprocessors seem to be rather less discerning than the average musician's hearing. Automatic looping might provide an instant solution, but in many cases it will not. Automatic looping is definitely desirable though, and it should at least provide a useful starting point for your own looping efforts.

Another form of instant fix for looping is some kind of crossfade feature. This is normally used as a last resort with an awkward sample that refuses to loop quietly. The basic idea is to do some averaging to reduce any differences between the end and beginning of the loop, so that a smoother transition is obtained. Some crossfade facilities work better than others, but this is always a very worthwhile feature to have available. Complex sounds can be all but impossible to loop without the aid of crossfading.

Looping for effect

Of course, sound samplers are not limited to straightforward mimicking of acoustic instruments, and they can be used to deliberately alter a sound in order to obtain special effects. A popular technique is to use a long loop of the type depicted in Fig.4.9. By looping back to the beginning of a sample a sort of echo effect can be obtained. In Fig.4.9 the loop is only applied over three cycles, but in practice the loop would probably be a few hundred cycles long. This effect is often used by vocalists to repeat one or two words over and over again. With this type of effect there is not usually too much difficulty in finding suitable points, as the (usually) sharp attack of the sound tends to mask any slight glitch. It works well when used with an envelope shaper to steadily fade out the sound.

Another simple technique is to play a loop backwards. Most instruments have an envelope shape with a short attack time and a relatively slow decay. The main effect of reversing a loop is to

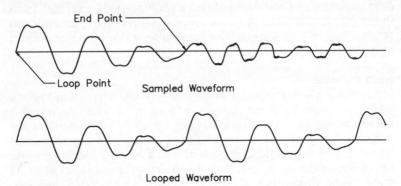

Figure 4.9 Looping can give a form of echo effect

reverse the envelope shape, giving what will often be a slow attack and a fast decay. This can give some weird sounds that sound surprisingly unlike the right-way-round sample.

Some samplers have a rotate facility. This basically involves starting the sample somewhere other than the beginning, and then looping round to the true beginning once the end of the sample has been reached. No doubt this can produce some good sounds, but it is a feature I have always found to be less than useful. This is certainly not true of an 'add' or 'overdub' facility. This merely enables one sound to be added on top of another. This seems to be a standard sampler feature, and one which usually permits any number of sounds to be added, one after another. In practice there is a limit to the number of sounds that can be accommodated, as each new sound effectively increases the recording level. You therefore have to record at a slightly lower than normal recording level when using this technique, so that sufficient headroom is left for all the sounds.

One way of using this facility is to give a simple chorus type effect. If you want (say) the sound of two or three flutes rather than just one, recording a flute sound two or three times in succession should give the desired effect. If you require something like strings plus further strings an octave lower, there is no need to have these on separate voices of an instrument. The two sounds can be recorded as a single sample and played on a single voice. It is quite feasible to play an entire orchestra on a single voice of a sampler, but this has limited practical application as the relative pitches of the instruments will remain constant, and there is no individual control over them. A point to bear in mind with complex samples is that the complexity of the waveform makes it very difficult to obtain really good looping. It is usually necessary to opt for a very long loop so that any slight and unavoidable glitch occurs as infrequently as possible, or crossfading (where it is available) can be more than a little helpful.

An extension of the 'add' facility is a form of crossfade which permits fading from one sample to another. In other words, you start with the sound of one instrument, and then fade this out while simultaneously fading in the sound of a second instrument. Some good original sounds can be produced in this way, with something like the twang of a guitar being faded into the more gentle sound of a flute.

Sound sources

A lot of the more way-out sampler sounds are not produced by any electronic manipulation of samples, but by recording non-instrument sounds. Things such as breaking glass, dripping taps, aircraft noise, and bird song can be used as the raw material for this type of thing. Remember that not all sounds have a definite pitch. With these noise sounds that do not have a definite pitch you are limited to using them for percussion parts. Sounds that do have pitch can be played in the normal way from the keyboard, but you will need to do some fine tuning in order to get the notes right. With non-instrument sounds you cannot usually select their pitch—you just have to take whatever tone happens to be produced. Most samplers seem to permit fine adjustment of the pitch so that these sounds can be used to play proper scales.

All the usual techniques can be applied to these sounds. In many cases they will be quite short sounds that will need to be looped in order to give a continuous sound. For this type of sampling it is more than a little helpful to have a sampler that has a good envelope shaper. The looped sound, which will probably have very little shape to its envelope at all, can then be shaped in normal synthesizer fashion. A lot of samplers seem to have an ADSR type envelope shaper, and a few have multi-stage types.

Synthesizer sampler

Another way of using a sampler to generate sounds, and sounds that do not have real origins, is to use some electronic means of generating the samples. This is by no means available on all samplers, although most can be loaded with samples via a MIDI link, and this gives the potential for generating samples on a computer and then loading them into the instrument. There are various ways in which a feature of this general type can operate.

One of the more common features amongst the more recently introduced samplers is the ability to draw a waveform and then have this converted into a sample that can be played back. A variation on this is the ability to redraw the waveform of part of an existing sample. These features obviously give tremendous potential for creating and modifying sounds.

Taking things a stage further, it is possible to have a system that enables the user to specify frequency components in a signal, with the microprocessor in the sampler (or an external computer) then doing the necessary mathematics to convert this information into the values for a sound sample. In other words, a sampler with this facility can operate as an additive synthesizer. In fact the same process can be applied to FM synthesis, and presumably other types of synthesis as well. The only major problem with this type of thing is that it can take quite a while for the microprocessor to work out all the values and load them into the sampler's memory. This can make the process of obtaining precisely the right sound a relatively long-winded one.

Obviously these systems greatly increase the music making potential of a sound sampler, and are likely to become increasingly common in the future.

In practice

If you understand the basic way in which a sampler functions, then there should be no real difficulty in producing good samples. On the other hand, it is something that is often not particularly easy either. It normally takes a reasonable amount of skill, and in some cases an unreasonable amount of patience as well. Ideally you should have a system that provides some means of visually displaying the sampled waveform. This generally means having a sampler that has some form of built-in graphics display (usually a liquid crystal type), or a computer plus a visual editor program for your sampler. Some samplers (notably the Roland S50, S550 and S330) have no built-in graphics display, but can be connected to an external monitor that provides a computer style display. This is very much the same as using a computer based visual editing package, but the computer and software are built into the sampler. This integrated approach is generally a bit faster and more convenient than using a separate computer and MIDI link.

Another alternative, and one which I have found to be quite useful, is to use an oscilloscope. An inexpensive oscilloscope could well be the cheapest solution with a sampler that has no built-in graphics display or output for a monitor, but you would probably need a certain amount of technical knowledge in order to use it properly.

First we will assume that no kind of waveform display is available. Of course, first of all you must record a sample at the correct level, and there will be some form of recording level indicator to help here. A few dummy runs should get the recording level just right. The other factor you need to consider at the recording stage is the sampling rate. Usually it is best to use the highest possible sampling rate, but this may give quite a short sampling time. If the sampling time at the highest sampling rate seems to be too short, then you will have to accept a lower rate and reduced bandwidth. Alternatively, you can settle for a short sample plus looping to sustain it. You have to make a subjective assessment as to which of these is best for the sound you are recording. For a fairly bright sound the looping method will probably be the most satisfactory. If a sound has little high frequency content, then there is little to lose by using a low sampling rate. In fact it could be advantageous to use a low sampling rate if a sound has no significant high frequency content. This will usually give a significantly lower background noise level than a higher sampling frequency. The reduced noise is due to the filter at the output of the sampler severely attenuating the high frequencies in the background hiss, which are the ones that are most noticeable.

Samplers almost invariably have automatic triggering. This is where the recording process starts automatically when an input signal above a certain threshold level is received. This threshold level should be adjustable, and results are normally best with it set at the lowest level that does not cause premature triggering. Setting this level too high will result in the initial part of the signal not being recorded, giving an unnatural attack to the sample when it is played back.

A modern trend is to have so-called 'psychic' sampling. This is where you can have the signal just prior to the trigger point added on to the beginning of a sample. With a sound that has a very fast attack this ensures that none of the all-important beginning of the sound is cut off. Taking things a stage further, you can sometimes operate a trigger button when the sound you wish to sample has just finished, and it will be faithfully recorded into the instrument's memory. This may all seem to be impossible, but it is much easier than you might think. The secret to the success of these systems is that the sampler is continuously recording and re-recording the incoming signal into its memory. In this way it can include in a sample any signals received shortly before the trigger signal.

Silent loops

With a short sample there is little option but to loop it in order to permit reasonably long notes to be provided. With a long sample this may be less crucial, but it is still normal to loop long samples in order to make sure that a long note is never cut short by the sample reaching its end point. With no waveform graphics to help select suitable loop points a lot of trial and error is needed. In order to get a really quiet loop it can take a lot of time, and this is certainly a job for those with endless patience.

If you start with the end of the sample as the end point of the loop, and set the loop point quite close to this, the looped signal will probably just be an unpleasant buzzing sound. Gradually moving the loop point further away from the end point will change the pitch of the buzz. At some stage the buzz will become quieter, and will become much closer to the pitch of the non-looped signal. It should also sound something not far removed from the sound of the non-looped signal. It is unlikely that it will sound good enough, with both an unacceptable error in pitch and buzzing caused by inaccuracies in the looping.

Moving the loop point further forward will cause a reintroduction of the large pitch shift and strong buzzing, and then it will start to subside again. You should find that moving the loop point steadily forward produces a succession of bad loop points with a few reasonably good ones mixed in with these and at (more or less) regular intervals. These good loop points are at approximately full cycles ahead of the end point. If you know that the good loop points are a certain number of sample values apart, you can quickly skip from one to the next in search of a really good one.

If you are lucky you will find a loop point that gives no significant change in pitch and which is free of clicks and buzzes. It is quite likely that you will not find a really good loop point first time though, and it is then a matter of moving the end point a little further forward and repeating the process. If this does not produce good results, move the end point a little further forward and try again. This process must be repeated until satisfactory loop and end points are located. With an awkward sample it is possible that no suitable points will be found. It is then a matter of sampling the sound again, and starting again in an attempt to find a good loop point. When you do find a good loop, try it over a range of notes. Loops often sound quite good on low notes but a little rough on high ones (or vice versa).

If your sampler has an automatic looping facility it is well worth giving it a chance. It may prove to be useless, but it is worth a try. A useful ploy with some auto-loop systems is to try them with various end points in an attempt to find one that is reasonably quiet. This will usually provide you with a reasonably good loop in fairly rapid time. Some manual adjustment of the loop point will often give improved results. Automatic looping systems often favour quite short loops, and manually setting longer ones by moving the loop point forward by a few cycles often gives a worthwhile improvement.

Waveform display

With the aid of some form of waveform display things are very much easier. A certain amount of patience is still required though. A waveform display enables you to pick out likely loop points, as you can see which points in the sample are whole cycles ahead of the end of the sample or your selected end point. You can also pick out an end point that is likely to give good results.

The often given advice is to look for end/loop points that are at the zero crossing point (i.e. where the signal goes from a positive to a negative value or vice versa). My experience does not uphold this view, and I have rarely found loops at the zero crossing point to give really good results. The waveform diagram of Fig.4.10 helps

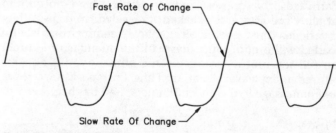

Fast Rate Of Change

Slow Rate Of Change

Figure 4.10 Looping is usually most successful at a point in the waveform where its amplitude is changing slowly

to explain this. Like a lot of acoustic instruments and other sound sources, the waveform is changing quite rapidly where it passes through the zero level. This means that there are quite high jumps in value from one input sample to the next, and the odds are very much against obtaining an accurate loop. Most waveforms have at least one section where they are relatively flat topped, and there is little change in value from one sample to the next. Looping on this part of a waveform gives a very much better chance of obtaining really quiet looping. Remember that obtaining a quiet loop is not the only problem. You must also use a long enough loop to avoid any significant change in pitch.

Disks

An important point to realise is that samplers do not normally have any battery back-up for their memory circuits. This is something that is not practical with the type of RAM chips used in most samplers. Consequently, when the instrument is switched off, the entire contents of its RAM are lost. A disk drive seems to be standard equipment for samplers. These take standard computer type disks (usually the 3.5 inch variety), or the 2.8 inch 'quickdisks' that seem to be unique to sound samplers. Samples are stored in magnetic form on these disks, using what is essentially the same method of recording used to record sounds onto cassette tapes etc. Any samples you wish to retain must be saved to disk prior to switching off the sampler, or moving on to a new sample for that area of memory. They can then be reloaded when required in just a matter of a few seconds. As well as the sample values, disks normally save and reload any other important data, such as end and loop points, envelope shaper parameters, etc.

Synthesizers normally have a substantial range of pre-programmed sounds built-in, with dozens more often available on plug-in cartridges. By contrast, sound samplers have no built-in sounds at all. Until a sample is taken, or loaded from disk, they have no music making ability at all. Playing a sampler that has no sample loaded will produce just noise, or the manufacturer might have designed the unit to produce some other sound. The Akai S700 produces a sinewave signal, and the Ensoniq Mirage gives you a spoken message to the effect that no sound has been loaded.

A sound library
If you want a good range of sounds from a sampler you must have a good library of disks for it. Some samples you will no doubt

produce yourself, but there will also be a range of factory disks available (and a few of these are normally supplied with the instrument). Some sets of factory disks are what could only be described as disappointing, while others are quite outstanding. Third party suppliers of samples may be a better proposition if you have an instrument which has a mediocre selection of factory disks. There are owners' clubs for some samplers, and these are often a valuable source of samples.

To produce your own disks you do not need to sample live instruments via a microphone. It is quite possible to record from tapes, records and compact disks. The latter is probably the best of these sources. Apart from its better quality technically, compact disk players make it very easy to locate and play the particular part of the piece you wish to sample. Recording very short snatches of copyright material is apparently quite legal incidentally (in the UK anyway). One problem with this type of sampling is that the instrument you wish to sample might be accompanied by other instruments which spoil the sample. The best chance of success is with small scale works and any pieces which have plenty of solo parts.

Pseudo synthesizer

A popular use of samplers is for sampling synthesizer sounds. One reason for doing this is that you may well know someone who has a synthesizer with some sounds that you particularly like and, assuming you own a sampler, sampling these sounds is cheaper than buying the particular synthesizer concerned! Another reason for doing this is that you can take samples from perhaps half a dozen synthesizers, and store them on disks. Taking a sampler and a box of disks around with you is a lot easier than having to lug around half a dozen synthesizers.

Something you should bear in mind is that samplers are much less versatile than synthesizers. With a synth, there are usually dozens of pre-programmed sounds, any of which are available at the touch of a button or two. Rapidly changing sounds, and going through a range of sounds is not normally a problem. With a sampler the number of available sounds is much more limited, and the only way of changing sounds might be to load a new one from disk. This does not usually take very long, but it is considerably less than instant.

117

PCM

The method of sampling described in this chapter is the usual form, but there are other methods. These are forms of pulse code modulation (PCM). Although these are forms of digital recording, they are substantially different to the method outlined previously. They are a form of single bit digital system, but they obtain a high level of performance. The most common form of pulse code modulation is the pulse width type.

We encountered pulse width modulation in an earlier chapter (see page 41). You may recall that the width of a pulse signal was varied by a low frequency oscillator. The higher the voltage from the low frequency oscillator, the longer the pulse duration. In this context, pulse width modulation works in much the same way, but the pulse signal is at a very high frequency that is well above the upper limit of the audio range. The modulating signal is the audio one that is to be recorded. There are various ways of storing the resultant pulse signal in memory, but the most simple one is to sample the pulse signal at very frequent intervals. The sampled logic levels are stored in memory that is only one bit wide rather than the usual byte or word-at-a-time approach. In order to accurately record the waveform, and thus obtain low noise and distortion levels, the sampling frequency must be very high indeed. Much higher in fact, than the maximum of 40 to 50kHz used in most conventional sampling systems. With only one-bit-wide memory required, but large amounts of it being gobbled up due to the very high sampling rate, this system does not require any less memory than a conventional sampling system of similar performance.

There is some advantage to this method of digital recording in that it requires relatively simple encoders and decoders. In particular, the decoder is very simple indeed. All that is required is a lowpass filter that could cost a matter of a few pence. The effect of this filtering is to smooth out the pulses to give a signal that is equal to the average output voltage. When the pulse width is wide a high output voltage is obtained — when it is narrow a low output voltage is obtained. This gives the reverse action of the modulation process, and recovers the original audio input signal.

As far as I am aware, no form of PCM is used in any sound sampler, past or present. It is used in some percussion synthesizers, and is also used for the sampled sounds of LA synths. For general use it probably suffers from difficulties with looping samples, but presumably a high quality PCM sound sampler would be perfectly feasible.

5 Choosing an instrument

For someone trying to decide which synth or sampler to buy, the choice is a difficult one. There are a large number of new instruments available, and an even greater variety of secondhand (or should it be 'pre-used') instruments on offer. Instruments from different manufacturers rely on different methods of synthesis, offer different features, and consequently do not all sound the same. There is a lot to be said for having a number of instruments from different manufacturers. You can then choose the best sounds from each one. The obvious drawback of this method is that, despite the relatively low cost of the current instruments, it is still too expensive for most users. On the other hand, a lot of users start off with a very modest music system, and with one thing leading to another, before too long find they have accumulated quite a lot of equipment. Most seem to consider that their money was well spent, and use all the equipment they own.

Cost effectiveness

Assuming that a modest start is to be made in the world of sound synthesis, with only a single instrument being bought, it would seem reasonable to either opt for an instrument that can provide a very wide range of sounds, or to choose one that has some sounds that you particularly like. The selection of any product is probably governed more by subjective judgments than objective ones, and this is certainly the case with musical instruments. Personal taste inevitably results in any instrument being loved by some and loathed by others. I doubt if there are any new synthesizers on sale today that are anything less than very good. The competition in the synth market is sufficiently strong to ensure that mediocre instruments do not survive long. I would still advise strongly against buying an instrument unless you have heard it in operation, and have had a reasonable opportunity to assess its sounds. The fact that it meets with the approval of the majority of the electronic music fraternity is no guarantee that you will like its sounds.

119

As with most things, in electronic music you generally get what you pay for. An expensive instrument will generally provide a wider range of sounds, and probably a better range of sounds than an inexpensive one. In fact a lot of the less expensive synthesizers are cut down versions of up-market models. For example, an inexpensive FM synth might have fewer operators than the more expensive models, and this difference will inevitably be reflected to some extent in their sounds.

If you are primarily interested in acoustic instrument sounds it might be worthwhile buying a sampler rather than a synthesizer. There seems to be a trend towards the use of sampled sounds in synthesizers, with Roland's LA technique currently being the best known method of this type. There are others which use similar techniques, and it seems likely that others will follow this trend. To some extent these systems give the best of both worlds, and instruments that use sampled sounds seem able to produce good acoustic instrument sounds, as well as good original and impressionistic sounds. It is important to realise though, that they do not have the flexibility of a sound sampler, in that you can only use the sampled sounds provided on-board the instrument. You cannot sample sounds yourself, or (in most cases) buy samples on disk for use with these instruments. Low cost instruments that utilize a mixture of synthesizer and sampling techniques offer what are arguably the best and widest range of sounds at the low cost end of the market.

Sampler costs

Low cost samplers are now very much cheaper than they were a few years ago, but are still somewhat more expensive than the cheapest synthesizers. I have used sound samplers a good deal, and they are my first choice for acoustic instrument sounds. However, there are difficulties when using sound samplers, and potential users should be aware of these.

Whereas synthesizers almost invariably come complete with a wide range of preprogrammed sounds, this is something that does not apply to sound samplers. Their range and quality of sounds is entirely dependent on the library of sound disks to support them. A few disks are normally supplied with a sound sampler, but these will probably only give you half a dozen or so sounds. The cheapest way of obtaining sound sample disks is to produce your own. You then only need a number of blank disks on which to record the samples. Of course, you can only produce your own samples if you can find suitable sounds to sample, and this may often prove to be impossible. This depends on the type of sounds you require, but it is something that often seems quite easy at the planning stage, but is very much more difficult when you start producing the samples. You may find a sound you want on a record or compact disk, but it will often be ruined by some other sound playing at the same time.

Producing good quality sound samples is a slow and painstaking business, and building up your own library could take a great deal of time. The cost is not negligible either. The exact cost is dependent on the type of disk your sampler uses, how many samples can be stored on each disk, the number of samples you require, and whether you bother with back-up disks (copies of the master disk which can be used if the original wears out or becomes damaged). The cost could be in excess of £100.

There is a reasonable range of factory disks available for most samplers, but the cost of using these is inevitably substantially greater than the do-it-yourself method. There are also independent companies that offer sample libraries for certain instruments. Using ready-made sample disks you can soon part with a few hundred pounds, but you will be able to get the instrument set up and ready to use in earnest almost immediately. There are user groups for some samplers, and good quality sample disks are available from some of these at relatively low cost. Also, some music shops have their own sample libraries which can be copied by customers, and this is something which could again save you a lot of time and money.

Features—can it do what you want it to?

The sounds produced by an instrument are of foremost importance for most musicians, but there are a lot of other factors that are also very important. Most instruments have one or two features missing from their specification, and at the low-cost end of the market there may well be a number of omissions and compromises. You need to check specification sheets to make sure that any facility that is of particular interest to you is there. If a feature is not mentioned in the specification for an instrument, then it almost certainly does not have it! Here is a list of standard synthesizer facilities, with a brief explanation for each one.

Polyphony

All the synthesizers and samplers currently available seem to provide polyphonic operation (i.e. they can play more than one note at a time). Some offer as much as 32 note polyphony (i.e. they can play up to 32 notes at once), but you often find that the maximum number of notes available depends on the complexity of the sounds being produced. Playing complex sounds, which in reality means practically any sound you are likely to use, might halve or even quarter the maximum number of notes that can be played at once. However, this should still leave a sufficient number of notes available. You are unlikely to play more than eight notes at once, although you should bear in mind that some sounds will have a fairly long release time. With these there is an advantage in having at least 16 note polyphony. Otherwise there is a risk of notes being terminated prematurely in order to make way for new notes.

Some instruments provide a 'layering' or 'stacking' facility that enables more than one sound at a time to be played. As one would expect, with two voices per note the maximum number of notes available is halved if this feature is used. The same is not usually true when key-split operation is used. This is where one zone of the keyboard plays one sound while the rest of the keyboard plays a different sound. There may be some restrictions though. With (say) an eight note polyphonic instrument the key-split might restrict the player to no more than four notes at once in each zone. A split such as three notes in one zone and five in the other might not be permitted.

Multi-timbral

This seems to be the latest buzzword in the world of electronic music. It merely means that a polyphonic instrument can have two or more different sounds at once, rather than having the same sound for each note. The key-split operation mentioned previously is an example of multi-timbral operation, and is the type normally used for live performances. There is an alternative form where (usually) each voice of an instrument has a separate sound, and the instrument is sequenced via MIDI, with each voice/sound on a separate MIDI channel. Using MIDI mode 4, this enables the instrument to effectively operate as a number of monophonic instruments, and with an eight to 16 voice instrument it is possible to produce some very complex sequences. With a 16 voice multi-timbral instrument you can effectively provide an entire orchestra with just the one instrument.

Many instruments go beyond MIDI mode 4 and offer an unofficial mode called 'multi' mode, 'special' mode, or some similar title. This differs from mode 4 in that each voice is not restricted to monophonic operation. With an eight voice instrument for example, it would be quite acceptable to have four note polyphony on one channel, and monophonic operation on four others. Some instruments have multi modes that are very flexible indeed. Something like eight note polyphony on eight channels might be provided, but with the proviso that no more than a certain number of notes (typically eight or 16) can play at any one time. If you intend to do any MIDI sequencing a multi mode option is more than a little useful.

Touch sensitivity
Most instruments now have at least basic touch sensitivity. This takes the form of a velocity sensitive keyboard, and this controls the envelope shaper. The peak level at the end of the attack period is only reached if a key is struck very hard. Striking a key less hard gives a lower peak signal level, and also reduces the signal's amplitude at later points in the envelope. In most cases all the envelope generators for a voice (including pitch and filter types) are controlled by the velocity at which keys are struck. A good touch sensitive system will have dozens of different volume levels, but some instruments only have about eight different levels. A large number of levels is clearly preferable, but a few levels is infinitely better than no touch sensitivity at all, and is adequate for most purposes.

It seems to be quite common for modern instruments to have adjustable touch sensitivity. With a low level of sensitivity the instrument provides virtually the same volume regardless of how hard the keyboard is played. With a high level of sensitivity a very wide dynamic range is available. This is useful for setting up an instrument to suit individual playing tastes, and the particular type of sound being played.

Aftertouch
Some synthesizers and samplers additionally implement some form of aftertouch. This is where pressing a key and holding it down hard produces an increase in volume, and reducing the pressure results in a drop in volume. This facility normally works on the sustain phase of the envelope shaper (and may affect any other envelope shapers for that voice). This tends to be looked on as something of a luxury feature, but it is an important one for

synthesizing the sounds of some acoustic instruments. With woodwind, string and many other instruments the player can vary the volume during the course of each note in practically any way he or she desires. The envelope shaper may permit quite complex envelopes to be used, but each note must use the same one. Aftertouch provides a means of controlling the volume of the instrument so that playing styles of acoustic instruments can be more faithfully copied. Where aftertouch is not implemented it might be possible to manually control the volume in some other way, such as using a swell pedal (which is effectively just a foot operated volume control). This is a relatively cumbersome way of handling the problem though, and might be inadequate in many cases.

There are two forms of aftertouch: polyphonic and channel (or voice, or overall) aftertouch. The polyphonic system is the more complex, and this has individual aftertouch for each key/note. Voice aftertouch has a sort of average value for all the notes that are playing on that particular voice of an instrument. Currently this seems to be the most common form of aftertouch. If you use an instrument for multi-timbral sequencing on MIDI mode 4, with each voice of the instrument on a different channel either form of aftertouch should provide separate aftertouch for each channel. For many purposes the overall form of this feature is perfectly adequate.

MIDI
MIDI is an involved subject, and is a system that has far greater capabilities than most people realise. Analogue synthesizers can be linked by their gate and CV sockets so that one instrument can control another, or a computer can control a synth via these inputs and a suitable interface unit. This system gives only limited control, has problems with a lack of true standardization, and requires a large number of connecting cables for polyphonic operation.

MIDI is a genuine standard, and there should be no difficulties if a MIDI system is built up using equipment from a variety of manufacturers. It permits a wide range of data types to be sent over a single connecting cable, including note information, program changes, synchronization signals, and aftertouch information. Obviously MIDI is not something that is of interest to everyone, but much modern electronic music seems to revolve around MIDI. It is an essential part of my own electronic music system.

It is important for budding MIDI musicians to realise that there is no universal MIDI implementation. MIDI sets down a standard for a whole range of features, but few (if any) instruments have a complete set. MIDI is not only applicable to instruments, and it can be applied to other pieces of equipment such as effects units and mixers. It is used on some quite basic and simple instruments as well as on some very expensive up-market models. Inevitably, some of the facilities included in MIDI are irrelevant to some pieces of equipment, either because they are of a fairly specialized nature, or because they are budget instruments that lack a lot of MIDI controllable features.

When setting up a MIDI system you need to check very carefully that the features you require are supported by the instruments you intend to buy. Also, some instruments have facilities that are not accessible from MIDI. This seems to be quite rare amongst modern instruments, where it is more likely that there will be features that are only accessible from MIDI. However, in the early days of MIDI some of the implementations were quite sparse. You need to be especially careful if you are contemplating the purchase of secondhand MIDI equipment that has its origins in the early days of MIDI. This means from 1982 to around 1985.

Obviously the sound quality of an instrument remains of paramount importance whatever the intended method of use. For MIDI applications the MIDI specification comes a close second though, and some aspects are of particular importance. Multi-timbral operation, MIDI mode 4, and 'multi' mode have already been discussed. These are important for most sequencing work, where you will probably wish to use a number of different sounds at once. The alternative to mode 4 or a multi mode is a number of synthesizers set to work on different channels, which is a superior but extremely expensive solution to the problem!

All the MIDI equipment I have encountered has been supplied with a MIDI chart which shows the MIDI messages that are recognized and those that are transmitted (there are often a number of differences between the two). This is something you need to study carefully in order to ascertain whether or not an instrument supports the features you require. Remember to read the small print which will usually detail any special feature (which includes any multi or special modes), as well as explaining any limitations of the implementation.

Sound modules
The current popularity of MIDI is demonstrated by the upsurge in the number of rack-mount sound modules that are now available.

In fact most instruments now seem to be released in both keyboard and rack-mount versions. The sound modules can be mounted in standard 19 inch wide equipment racks, but most users simply stack them one on top of the other (not to be recommended if you have a lot of them). These modules can only be played via their MIDI interfaces, and the general idea is to have one keyboard instrument in the system which is then used to play any desired instrument, or to record data into a computer when real-time sequencing.

Apart from the obvious advantage of avoiding the high cost of one keyboard per instrument, it also saves a great deal of space. This is an important factor for those of us with spare-bedroom studios. Obviously the MIDI specification is all-important with a unit of this type, where every feature it possesses should ideally be available via MIDI messages.

Disk drive
A disk drive is standard equipment for a sound sampler, where masses of data must be loaded into the instrument before it can be used. As a disk drive is a fairly expensive item, it is not usually included on synthesizers where relatively small amounts of data must be stored and retrieved. Synthesizers normally have some built-in RAM which is used to store sets of parameters for the various sounds programmed into the instrument. Although RAM loses its contents when it is disconnected from its power source, the amounts of RAM used in synthesizers are generally quite small. This makes it feasible to use a battery back-up system, where a long-life battery supplies power to the RAM when the instrument is switched off. Provided the right type of RAM is used, it will have an extremely low power consumption under stand-by conditions, and a long battery life can be obtained. In most cases the battery life is determined by the shelf life of the battery, rather than how quickly it is run down by the RAM. A life of five years or more is usually achieved.

There is only a limited amount of on-board RAM, and a limit to the number of sounds that can be stored in it. There is normally some form of memory expansion available, which usually means plug-in cartridges. This is a very quick and easy way of storing sound data, but it is not necessarily very cheap. If a very large library of sounds must be stored it is a decided asset to have a disk drive. These usually take standard 3.5 inch disks, and can store either 360k or 720k of data, depending on whether they use one or both sides of the disk. The amount of data per sound varies enormously from one instrument to another, but would normally be under 1k. Each disk can potentially hold a large number of sets of sound data, and at a cost of only about £1.50 per disk.

Something I would warn against is spending large amounts of time amassing thousands of sets of sound data and (or) samples for a sound sampler. It is very easy to end up in the position where you are spending all your time setting up the system and are left with no time for actually using it. This is analogous to the hi-fi buffs who spend all their time listening to the technical quality of the system and making adjustments, but never really listen to the music. It might be an interesting hobby, but at best it is rather missing the point!

Effects

Add-on effects units are covered in the next chapter. Some instruments have several built-in effects, and these are obviously a useful bonus which could save the cost of an external effects unit. An integral chorus unit is useful for producing good string section sounds etc., and this method often seems to work better than dual detuned oscillators. A few instruments now have a built-in digital reverberation unit, which is a very worthwhile addition. An add-on digital reverberation unit is usually quite expensive. One slight problem with a built in unit of this type is that it will probably only be able to apply the effect to its own sounds. Due to the way in which this internal effect is usually obtained, processing external signals is not feasible. This can limit the usefulness of built-in reverberation if an instrument is to be used in a multi-instrument setup.

Mixing it

Another increasingly common feature is some form of built-in audio mixer. This enables the output of each voice to be mixed into a stereo output signal. Again, there is usually no provision for processing external signals. In a multi-instrument system you will still need a mixer to combine the outputs of the instruments into a single stereo channel. However, internal mixing can limit the amount of external mixing that is required, so that a simple and inexpensive mixer can be used where an up-market unit might otherwise be required. Usually a built-in mixer is controlled via the usual push-button switches with a liquid crystal display to show the settings. This is more cumbersome than the standard mixer slider controls, but is adequate where preset mixing levels are all that are needed.

Some instruments offer separate outputs for each voice instead of (or possibly in addition to) integral audio mixing. This is a very useful feature if you wish to mix a multi-timbral output down into a stereo output signal, and is a popular feature amongst those who indulge in MIDI sequencing. It is preferred by many to built-in mixing, but personally, I am quite happy to settle for built-in mixing wherever possible.

Display

Modern instruments make extensive use of data entry via push buttons with a display of some kind being used to show what parameter is being adjusted and what its current value is. The success of this system is largely dependent on how logically (or otherwise) things are arranged, and how much information the display can provide. Judging how well the controls are organized is something you can only do after using an instrument for a while. Displays are less subjective. A large liquid crystal display is preferable to a LED or liquid crystal type which can only display a few digits. This is something which seems to be much better on modern instruments than those from a few years ago.

Some displays now provide some graphics capability. This is a very welcome development which can make it very much easier when setting envelope shapes. It is also a great asset for a sound sampler where it can provide a built-in waveform display that can make finding suitable loop points a very much easier task.

6 Effects units

Effects units seem to be primarily the domain of guitarists. The single sound of a guitar can be changed in various ways by a battery of effects units such as distortion boxes, metal pedals, and flangers. Many of these are irrelevant to the synthesist who can obtain a fair proportion of these effects, or something broadly comparable, simply by setting up the synth in the appropriate manner. While many effects units are of little value to the synthesizer user, it would be a mistake to overlook them completely. There are some that can provide effects that are not available on a synthesizer, unless it happens to have the effect concerned built-in. It is noticeable that integral effects units such as chorus and reverberation are much more common now than was once the case.

Delay

The more simple effects units such as distortion units and metal pedals are the ones that are least likely to be of any use to a synthesist. If you want a lot of distortion on the output signal, you simply choose a waveform that has plenty of harmonic content. If you require metal sounds, you only need to switch in the synthesizer's ring modulator. Chorus, echo and reverberation are the types of effect that cannot easily be produced without an effects unit designed specifically for that purpose, and are therefore of more value to the synthesizer user.

These three types of effects unit are all based on a delayline. This is a circuit that takes in a signal, and supplies an identical version at the output, but delayed in time by a certain amount. For musical effects the required delay time is usually between about 1 millisecond and one second. There are many different types of delayline, but only two types are commonly used in musical effects units. These are the analogue CCD (charge coupled device) and digital types. In the past CCD types have been the most common, primarily because they could be built using relatively cheap components. More recently digital effects units have started to become more common, and many of the devices on which the CCD types are based have gone out of production. It seems likely that digital delaylines will dominate in the near future.

Digital delay

If you understand the fundamentals of sampling, there should be no difficulty in grasping the basic way in which a digital delayline functions. Like a sampler, the input signal is fed to an analogue-to-digital converter, and then stored in RAM in digitized form. The first value is stored in RAM location 1, or 'address' 1 in the normal computer terminology. Subsequent values are stored at addresses 2, 3, 4, etc. When the unit runs out of RAM it simply goes back to the beginning and stores the subsequent values at addresses 1, 2, 3, etc., over-writing all the values it just stored at these addresses. It cycles in this manner indefinitely, continuously writing values into memory.

The delay is obtained by reading values from the RAM just before they are over-written by new ones. The system will have written values to every RAM address before getting back to any given value and reading it out into the digital to analogue converter. This obviously gives a delay between a value being written into RAM and read out again. The more RAM the unit has, the longer each loop takes, and the longer the delay that is obtained. With a sampler the length of a sample is governed by the amount of RAM available, and the sampling frequency. The same rules apply to digital delay lines, and the delay time can be altered by increasing or decreasing the sample rate. It can also be changed by using less than the full amount of RAM. Another option is to read the values well before they are over-written rather than at the very last instant prior to obliteration.

Also in common with sampling, a low clock rate is unusable because it provides an inadequate bandwidth, and high resolution is needed in order to obtain low levels of noise and distortion.

An advantage of digital delaylines over their analogue counter-parts is that they can provide very low levels of noise and distortion even with a very long delay time. In fact the length of the delay has no effect on the audio quality of the system. This is dependent on the number of bits used, the sampling frequency, and how close to perfection the circuits can manage to come. A 16 bit system with a sampling rate of 40 to 50kHz can therefore provide delays as long as required together with compact disk quality. However, a system of this type needs expensive analogue-to-digital and digital-to-analogue converters, and a large amount of RAM. Really good digital delaylines are quite expensive, especially when compared to the prices of the bargain synthesizers that are now available. A good digital effects unit could easily cost substantially more than the cheaper synthesizers.

Bucket brigades

Analogue delaylines use CCD integrated circuits, or 'bucket brigade' devices as they are often called. The way in which these work has some similarities to the way in which digital delaylines function, but there are also substantial differences. These devices have what are a form of memory cell, but an analogue type. These are very simple components called capacitors, and if a capacitor is charged to a certain voltage, it retains that charge voltage indefinitely. In practice the voltage will die away over a period of time, but in a delayline application the charge will normally only be stored for about a second or less. There should be very little droop in the charge voltage during such a short period of time.

The basic setup is to have a series of capacitors linked by electronic switches. The first capacitor is connected to the input, and it rapidly charges up to the input voltage. It is then connected to the next capacitor in the chain, causing it to pass on its charge to this second stage of the circuit. Then the first capacitor is connected back to the input, and it adjusts to the new input voltage. At the same time, capacitor number 2 passes on its charge to capacitor number 3. This process continues with new input samples being taken repeatedly and passed on down the chain of capacitors. This is analogous to buckets of water being passed along a human chain, and it is from this that the 'bucket brigade' term is derived.

Eventually the samples reach the last stage of the device, and it is from this that the output signal is taken. It obviously takes a certain amount of time for the samples to pass right through the device and to reach the output. The more capacitors in the chain, the longer the delay time. In common with digital delaylines, the delay time is also proportional to the sampling rate used.

There is an inherent advantage in analogue delaylines in that they have infinite resolution. The output signal is a stepped type, like the output from a digital audio circuit, but the output voltages are exactly the same as the input voltages that were sampled. No rounding up or rounding down errors occur. In theory an analogue delayline can have zero noise and distortion levels.

In reality the situation is very different. The signal undergoes a lot of processing between the input and output of a circuit of this type. The longer the delay time, the more stages that are required, and the more processing that occurs. As a result of this CCD integrated circuits produce significant amounts of noise and distortion. The distortion is not generally very high, and is usually under 1%. This falls some way short of true hi-fi performance, but is adequate for most electronic music applications. The noise level can also be quite low. In my experience of these devices, a high sampling rate usually provides an excellent signal to noise ratio. Unfortunately, in many applications it is necessary to opt for a fairly low sampling frequency. CCD devices generally only have around 500 to 3500 delaying stages. As a stage cannot simultaneously collect a sample from the previous stage and pass on its sample to the next stage, there are only half as many samples as capacitors in the circuit. This effectively gives only about 250 to 1750 delaying stages. Reasonably long delay times can only be obtained by using low sampling rates. Of course, two or more of these devices can be connected in series so that a cumulative delay is provided, but this also gives cumulative noise and distortion! CCD delaylines are often used in conjunction with compander noise reduction systems in order to obtain an acceptably low background noise level.

Chorus

The chorus effect is one of the more simple delayline types, and one which is usually based on an analogue delayline. The usual setup is one along the lines shown in Fig.6.1.

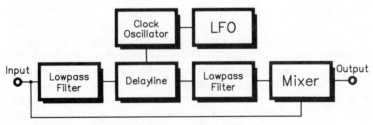

Figure 6.1 The arrangement used in a chorus unit

The lowpass filter at the input of the unit is needed to combat aliasing distortion, which affects analogue sampling systems, not just digital types. The lowpass filter at the output removes the steps in the signal. These steps will contain high frequencies outside the passband of the delayline, and should be almost totally removed from the output signal. A mixer is fed with the delayed and non-delayed signals.

With a fixed delay, the effect of the unit depends on the delay provided. With a very short delay the effect will be negligible. With a delay of about 10 to 60 milliseconds the two signals will be heard as separate signals, and the effect will be that of a doubling up of the instruments fed into the unit. Feed one guitar sound into the unit, and the output will give the effect of two guitars playing in unison. A delay of more than about 60 milliseconds again gives two signals that are heard as separate sounds, but they are perceived as an original sound and an echo of that sound. For the chorus effect it is therefore a delay of around 10 to 60 milliseconds that is required.

In order to give a richer chorus effect it is normal for the delay time to be varied. The rate at which samples are taken and passed along the chain of capacitors is controlled by a clock oscillator. In order to vary the delay time it is merely necessary to use a voltage controlled oscillator to provide the clock signal, and to frequency modulate it with a low frequency oscillator.

The effect of this varying of the delay time is a little more complex than you might think. When the delay time is being decreased, samples will be sent out from the output faster than they were taken in at the input. This is due to the clock rate having increased during the time that the samples have been making their journey through the circuit. The result of this is a rise in the pitch of output signals. This increase is matched by a reduction in the pitch of output signals as the delay time is increased, and the clock rate is slowing down. A delayline can therefore be used to provide vibrato, although this is not usually of any interest to synth users who can obtain this effect in a much simpler way.

In a chorus unit, matters are a little more complex than this, due to the mixing of the delayed and non-delayed signals. Normally if two identical signals are mixed they simply add together to form a stronger version of the signal. In this case there is the complication that the signals are not quite the same in that one is lagging behind the other slightly. At some frequencies the signals will be in-phase and will add together, while at other frequencies they will be out-of-phase and will cancel out one another to some extent. This produces peaks and troughs in the frequency response, and the result of varying the delay time is to sweep these anomalies in the response. The depth of modulation controls the extent to which the peaks and troughs are swept.

With this doubling-up effect, the vibrato on the delayed signal, and the swept filtering, a chorus unit provides what is quite a complex effect. It is similar to using a twin VCO synthesizer with the two oscillators on slightly different frequencies. Using vibrato on one of the VCOs gives an even more similar effect. To my ears anyway, the two effects do not sound quite the same though.

Whether either of these methods can really turn a single violin sound into the sound of a full string section is debatable. Adding a chorus effect to most single instrument sounds certainly gives a much richer sound, and it is a very worthwhile effect. Most users find its ensemble producing qualities quite convincing. Using the twin VCO method plus a chorus unit seems to give even better results. However, provided the looping problems can be overcome, sampling now offers what is probably an even more convincing way of obtaining these types of sound.

The only drawback I have found with chorus units is that a normally very quiet instrument can suddenly exhibit a much higher background noise level once the chorus effect is added. This is presumably due to the use of a CCD delayline having a low clock frequency range in order to give suitably long delays, and not having the benefit of compander noise reduction. With a lot of effects units that use delaylines you find that the straight-through signal has the full audio bandwidth, while the delayed signal has what in many cases is a rather restricted upper frequency response figure due to the use of a low clock frequency. The upper limit of the frequency response is as little as 4kHz or thereabouts in some cases.

This is not as bad as you might think, as it is the unprocessed part of the signal that is the more important in this respect. If this has low distortion and the full frequency range, the overall quality will probably be quite acceptable. A delayed signal of restricted bandwidth will not grossly detract from the audio quality, although the full bandwidth from the whole signal is obviously still preferable.

Chorus units normally have some user-adjustable controls. As a minimum there should be a chorus amount control. This merely controls the amount of delayed signal that is mixed in with the unprocessed signal, and it therefore controls the strength of the effect. Controls for the LFO rate and depth may also be provided, and where these are available it is well worthwhile experimenting with various settings to find one that gives the effect which is most suitable for the type of signal you are processing. Extreme settings can sometimes give some interesting (if less than natural) chorus effects.

Phasing

Phasing and chorus are two effects that seem to cause a certain amount of confusion. Although they are generated in a similar fashion they are not the same, and to my ears at least, sound quite different. The basic scheme of things for the phasing effect is much the same as the chorus arrangement of Fig.6.1, but the delayline and its associated stages are replaced with a series of phase shifters.

A phase shifter is a fairly simple circuit that provides a phase lag that is frequency dependent. With the signal passed through a chain of these and then mixed with the unprocessed signal, the result is similar to that obtained with a chorus unit. At some frequencies the signals are in-phase, while at others they are out-of-phase. Peaks and troughs in the frequency response are produced, and by controlling the phase shifters from the LFO, these peaks and troughs can be swept up and down in frequency.

This effect differs from the chorus one in that there is no delayed signal, only a phase-shifted signal which is not quite the same. The phase shifted signal will not be heard as a separate sound source. Also, there is no significant vibrato on the phase shifted signal. It therefore provides what is a very much milder effect. Whereas a chorus effect is normally quite noticeable even on the most simple of input signals, phasing can be less than immediately apparent on signals that do not contain a broad spectrum of frequencies. It is more effective on something like a bright bowed bass string sound than on a flute sound. Phasing is particularly effective with noise-based sounds.

Like most effects units, the sound it produces is difficult to describe. The processed and unprocessed signals are normally mixed in such a way that notches of very deep attenutation are produced at the out-of-phase frequencies. Together with strong modulation from the LFO this gives a sort of swept hollow sound that can provide some weird effects. Phasing can be used with reduced sweep range and less pronounced peaks/notches in the frequency response, but it generally needs to be used at something approaching the maximum settings in order to have a really noticeable effect. It is an effect that is probably better suited to space sounds than to a pseudo band or orchestra.

Flanging

This is a variation on the chorus effect, but it can produce a much stronger effect, and is decidedly less subtle. With the chorus effect the sound is made much richer, but it retains most of the character of the original. Flanging can drastically alter a sound.

Flanging is produced using the same circuit elements that are utilized in a chorus unit, but they are rearranged slightly, as shown in Fig.6.2. Basically this just boils down to moving the mixer stage

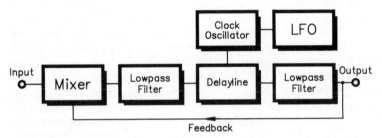

Figure 6.2 Rearranging the circuit blocks of a chorus unit gives a flanger

from the output to the input. This changes things more than you might expect though, and the point to note is that some of the delayed signal is fed back to the input of the unit. As a result of this, some of the signal circulates around the system for a while before it decays to an inaudible level. This produces a very complex effect which has elements of just about every type of effects unit known to man!

In terms of its sound, flanging has what is unmistakably a form of swept filtering sound, but it is equally obviously much more than this. It gives what I would term a 'brittle' or 'spiky' sound which lacks the smoothness of the 'swooshing' sounds produced by phasing. Like phasing it is at its best with a signal that contains a broad spectrum of frequencies. Also in common with phasing, it is definitely better suited to 'space' sounds and the like rather than normal instrumental sounds. The effect can be varied to a considerable extent by adjusting the modulation frequency, modulation depth, and the amount of feedback. Flanging is generally used to produce quite a strong effect, but like any powerful musical effect, you should avoid the temptation to use it excessively.

There is no straight-through signal with the flanging effect, and because of this it is important for it to be provided by a good quality delayline. This is all the more important due to the use of feedback. This circulates noise around the system, and gives an increased noise level.

Reverberation

This currently seems to be one of the most popular effects amongst synth users. When music is played in a large hall, the sounds tend to bounce around the walls, ceiling, floor, and are also bounced off objects within the room. Sounds that take the direct route to your ears arrive more quickly than those that do a few laps of a large hall first. In fact sounds will arrive via a multitude of routes, with each one taking a different time. This smears sounds over a period of time, with you first hearing the direct sound, and then the reflected sounds that gradually die away. These reflected signals are not normally heard as distinct echoes, because there are a large number of them following one after another in very rapid succession. This gives a jumbled and indistinct sound. An echo is produced when there is only one reflective surface, and only one reflection of the sound. No doubt most musicians are very familiar with the 'warm' sound produced by the multitude of reflected signals in a large hall, or the 'reverberation' as it is termed.

Although reverberation is generally associated with large halls, it is something that is present in practically every room. In general, the larger a room, the longer it takes for the reverberation to die away to an insignificant level. There are other factors which determine the reverberation time, and one of these is how well the interior of the building and its contents reflect sound waves. Most walls and ceilings are good reflectors of sound, but carpeted floors, soft furnishings, and people tend to absorb sound. The acoustics of an empty hall can be quite different to those obtained when it is full of people. Adding people generally shortens the reverberation time.

Mechanical reverb
In the past the main methods of producing reverberation were electro-mechanical. The most common method was the springline type. A typical springline unit consists of two long springs, side

by side, and having a transducer at each end. Feeding an electrical signal into one transducer results in it producing sound waves that travel relatively slowly down the springs. When these waves reach the far end of the springs they are reflected back down them, and they are repeatedly reflected up and down the springs until they subside. The two springs have slightly different characteristics so that their delay times (i.e. the time taken for the wave to do one length of the springs) are different. The second transducer picks up the sound waves from the springs and converts them back into electrical signals. These are mixed with the unprocessed signal to add a reverberation effect to it.

For such a crude method this type of reverberation unit sounds remarkably good. It tends to give a rather 'coloured' effect though, and units of this type often suffer from microphony. This is where the second transducer acts as a sort of microphone that picks up any loud noise or vibration in the vicinity of the unit. There can even be problems with acoustic 'howl-around'. Superior results can be provided by an improved version called a 'plate' reverberation unit, which uses a metal plate instead of the springs. These have never achieved widespread use due to their relatively high cost.

Electronic reverb
Modern reverberation units achieve a very convincing effect, and are based on delaylines (either analogue or digital). They use a setup of the type shown in Fig.6.3. Here the input signal is taken to a mixer, then to another mixer, and then through to the output.

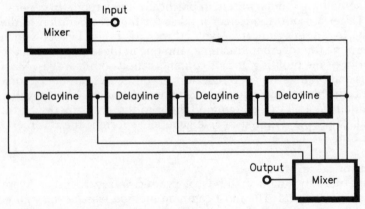

Figure 6.3 Reverberation effect schematic

Some of the input signal is used to drive a series of delaylines, and their outputs are fed to the mixer at the output of the unit. The delaylines provide different delay times, and usually each one provides a slightly longer delay than its predecessor. In practice it is really one long delayline that is used, but in the case of an analogue type it has outputs from various stages, not just the last one. For a digital delayline it is a matter of having several digital to analogue converters, with one operating a number of memory addresses ahead of the one that provides the full delay, the next one operating a number of addresses ahead of that one, and so on.

At the output this gives a direct signal plus delayed signals that are analogous to reflected signals in a hall. However, even with (say) a dozen taps on the delayline, this gives far too few 'reflected' signals. This problem is overcome by feeding some of the output from the delayline back to the mixer at the input. The input signal therefore circulates around the system, dropping slightly in level on each circuit until it dies away to an insignificant level. This effectively boosts the number of reflected signals by a substantial amount, and gives a vastly improved effect. As there are no transducers to pick up sounds and vibrations, this method is free from problems with microphony. Mechanical means of producing reverberation tend to result in quite large pieces of equipment, but this all-electronic method requires no large components.

A reverberation unit based on an analogue delayline can produce quite a good effect, but the fairly long delay time required is stretching the ability of these circuits. Digital delaylines can provide excellent results, but unfortunately they are quite expensive at present. Most units, whether based on an analogue circuit or a digital one, permit the amount of feedback to be adjusted. This controls the reverberation time, with a large amount of feedback providing a long reverberation time. Often the delay times will also be adjustable. For short reverberation times a much better effect is obtained if the delay time is reduced and the feedback level is kept quite high, rather than keeping a long delay time and using little feedback. There is usually a reverberation level control, and this simply controls the strength of the reverberation signal relative to the main signal. Often there are preset settings available, and you just select the desired type of room (large room, small hall, etc.).

In the mix

Much electronic music is recorded by connecting the outputs of instruments direct to a tape recorder. This has advantages over connecting an instrument to an audio system and then recording it via a microphone. Apart from being a lot easier, it gives a higher quality recording technically. It gives rather flat results in that there is no natural reverberation at all on the recorded signal. The only reverberation that will be obtained is any that is produced by the room in which the recording is played, and this will often be negligible. Modern furnishings tend to have excellent sound absorbing qualities, and the average lounge has a very short reverberation time. It is for this reason that reverberation has always been a popular effect with synth users, and probably always will be.

Most users these days like to produce a stereo output from their instruments. Stereo outputs on instruments are now quite a common feature, as are individual outputs for each voice so that you can do your own stereo mixing. It is debatable whether mixing the outputs of electronic instruments into stereo channels produces a true stereo signal, or an artificial stereo effect. Real stereo is produced, at its most basic level, by having two microphones, one on the left hand side of the stage and one on the right hand side. Instruments on the left and right hand sides of the stage are picked up more strongly by their respective microphones, while instruments in the middle are received more or less equally by both microphones.

During playback of the stereo signal the two channels are fed to two loudspeakers placed a few metres apart. Due to what could be described as an aural illusion, sounds that are stronger from the left hand speaker seem to come from the left of the sound stage, those that are loudest from the right hand speaker seem to emanate from the right hand side of the sound stage, and those that are equally strong from both speakers seem to originate in the middle of the sound stage. In other words, the original sound stage is reproduced by stereo recording and playback.

In electronic music systems a mixer is used to place the output signal of each instrument (or each voice of a multi-timbral instrument) in each stereo channel at the required level. The usual arrangement is an overall level control that sets the volume of the signal in both channels, and a pan control. The latter is used to place instrument or voice at the required position in the stereo sound stage. If you set this control just left of centre, then that is where the instrument on that channel of the mixer should appear in the sound stage. Not all stereo mixers have monophonic inputs and pan controls, but you can obtain much the same effect by connecting the input signal to both channels of a stereo input. The balance control then effectively becomes the pan control.

This type of mixing produces a stereo signal that is artificial in that there is no original sound field to reproduce. On the other hand, it is not that far removed from the way in which most stereo recordings are produced these days. Instead of a two microphone setup, there is normally a microphone for each instrument or group of instruments. A large mixing desk is then used to mix down all these signal sources into a stereo signal. In effect, a number of monophonic sources are being mixed to produce a stereo signal, just as in an electronic music system.

There is a difference in that in the 'real' recording setup there will be some pick up by each microphone of instruments other than the ones it is directed at, plus some pick up of the reverberation in the recording studio. To a large extent the recording will therefore reflect the natural acoustics of the studio, which is an element that will obviously be lacking in an all electronic recording. However, some added reverberation and a well mixed recording can give some very realistic results. I have occasionally played people some demonstration pieces of this kind, only to be disbelieved when I have revealed that there is no hall, no musicians, only electronic instruments controlled by a computer!

The rest

An echo unit is, as one would probably expect, another effects unit that is based on a delayline. The delayed and unprocessed signals are simply added in order to give a single echo. For a multiple echo effect it is merely necessary to use some feedback. The greater the feedback level, the more echoes that are obtained before they die away to zero. The delay time of the delayline does, of course, set the time between echoes.

You need to be a little careful when using an echo unit with a lot of feedback. With signals being circulated around the system for a long time and new signals arriving, it is possible for the signal level to build up to the point where overloading and clipping of the output signal occur. Large amounts of feedback work best with brief and intermittent input signals.

It is worth pointing out that some synthesizers can produce an echo effect by giving short repetitive bursts of signal. Unfortunately, this useful capability is something that is far from being a universal feature. One way of achieving it is to use a pulse LFO signal to heavily amplitude modulate the VCO. This chops up the output signal into short bursts, and the envelope generator is then used to give the required decay characteristic. With a multistage envelope shaper it might be possible to set this up to give a similar effect. Where this is possible this is probably the better method. It is likely to give more predictable results than the LFO method.

The waa-waa effect is produced using a swept lowpass filter having strong resonance. This is something that can be obtained on many synthesizers without any external assistance. The same is true of vibrato, distortion, envelope shaping effects, and tremolo.

Appendix 1: Glossary

Additive synthesis
All sounds are made up from sinewaves, which are pure tones that have a single component frequency. Additive synthesis uses sinewaves to build up the required waveform. If each sinewave source has its own envelope generator, the wave shape can be varied in any desired manner during the course of the sound. In theory, additive synthesis can be used to generate any sound.

ADSR
The standard form of envelope shaper. Its adjustable parameters are attack rate (A), decay rate (D), sustain level (S) and release rate (R). Some older synthesizers have a more simple attack/decay envelope shaper, but most modern instruments have more complex multi-stage types (like the eight stage Casio envelope generators).

Algorithm
In an electronic music context this usually means a particular way of connecting together the basic sound generating units ('operators') of an FM synthesizer. 'Carriers' are operators that directly contribute to the audio output of the synthesizer, while 'modulators' are used to frequency modulate the carriers so as to produce a more complex output signal from them.

Amplitude
The amplitude of a signal is a measure of its voltage. In terms of the sound produced by an instrument, amplitude corresponds to its loudness.

Amplitude modulation
This simply means using one signal to vary the amplitude (volume) of another. Using an LFO to amplitude modulate the output of a synthesizer gives the standard tremolo effect.

Analogue
An analogue quantity is one that can have absolutely any value. Virtually everything in the 'real world' is analogue—a piece of string can be cut to any length. Much modern electronics deals in digital signals, where only a certain series of values are allowed. A piece of digital string would be one that could be cut to any length provided it was a whole number of (say) metres. Provided a digital system has a high enough resolution (i.e. its minimum increments are small enough) its digital nature will not detract from its performance. In fact the best digital audio circuits now seem able to out-perform the best analogue circuits in most respects.

Analogue-to-digital converter
Many electronic musical instruments have largely digital circuits, but the 'real world' deals in analogue quantities. The purpose of an analogue-to-digital converter is to take in real signals and convert them into a form that digital circuits can deal with. For example, a converter of this type is needed in a sound sampler to change the varying voltage from the microphone into a form that is suitable for storage in the instrument's digital memory circuits. A digital-to-analogue converter is used to convert digital signals back into analogue form so that they can be handled by ordinary amplifiers, loudspeakers, etc.

Aperiodic
An aperiodic waveform is one that is non-repetitive. Consequently it does not have a definite pitch, and is what would more commonly be termed a form of noise signal.

Attack
An envelope shaper parameter. This is the first stage of the envelope, and is usually the rate at which the signal climbs to its peak level (or in some cases a level specified by the user).

Attenuate
If a signal is attenuated it is reduced in level. A VCA can be used to attenuate an entire signal—a VCF will attenuate some frequencies and leave others unaffected.

Balanced modulator
An alternative name for a ring modulator (also known as a double balanced modulator).

Bandpass filter
This is a filter that permits only frequencies over a narrow band to pass unattenuated. Frequencies above and below this passband are attenuated.

Beat note
An interaction between two signals on almost the same frequency produces a throbbing sound. This throbbing is at a frequency which is equal to the difference between the frequencies of the two signals causing the interaction. This (usually sub-audio) frequency is the beat note.

Bit
This is a contraction of 'binary digit'. In other words, a single digital signal which can only be logic 0 or logic 1.

Break point
This can be used to describe the point at which a keyboard is split, but it can also be applied to a filter to describe its cutoff frequency.

Byte
A set of eight digital bits. Single bits are of little use for most applications, and a set of eight bits is the basic digital building block. The bits are used together to provide a range of values from 0 to 255 (decimal), or 00000000 to 11111111 in binary.

Carrier
This is an operator in an FM synthesizer that has its output connected to the audio output of the instrument. It can therefore be heard directly, unlike a modulator which can only be heard indirectly via the effect it has on a carrier.

Chip
A name often used to describe an integrated circuit (which is based on a chip of silicon). These are the components that do most of the work in modern instruments, and permit such advanced designs to be produced in such compact and inexpensive forms.

Chorus
An effect which takes the signal from a single instrument and produces an output that sounds like a number of instruments playing in unison. This is sometimes known as the 'ensemble' effect.

Clock
Most digital circuits are controlled by an electronic circuit that provides a regular train of electrical pulses. This is the clock oscillator, or just 'clock' as it is often termed.

Contour generator
A term that is a little used alternative to envelope generator.

Control voltage (CV)
Analogue synthesizers have as many of their circuits as possible under voltage control. This enables one section of an instrument to modulate another, such as using a low frequency oscillator to modulate a VCO in order to produce the vibrato effect. Any voltage that is used to control a VCO, VCA, etc. is a control voltage. Most analogue synthesizers have a 1 volt per octave CV characteristic.

Cosine wave
This is the same as a sinewave, but it is one that lags another signal by 90 degrees (i.e. one quarter of a cycle).

Cutoff frequency
This is the frequency at which a highpass or lowpass filter starts to take effect. It is sometimes used to describe the operating frequency of a notch or bandpass filter, but these really have what should be termed a centre frequency rather than a cutoff frequency.

Cycle
A soundwave has first a rise in pressure from the normal level to a peak value, then a fall in pressure to a negative peak, and finally a rise in pressure back to the normal level. This is one cycle, but a continuous sound has many cycles occurring one after the other.

DCA
This is a digital controlled amplifier. In most cases this is a VCA with a digital-to-analogue converter added ahead of its control input. This enables it to be easily integrated into a modern digital instrument.

DCF
A digital controlled filter (DCF) is sometimes just a VCF plus a digital to analogue converter to permit digital control. However,

some filters are truly digital, or use a combination of digital and analogue techniques.

DCO
This stands for 'digital controlled oscillator'. This is not normally an oscillator in the conventional sense, but a complex digital circuit that can produce very complex output waveforms. Most modern synthesizers have DCOs in place of the VCOs.

DCW
DCW (digital controlled wave) circuits are used in Casio's PD synthesizers, and are a sort of pseudo-VCF. They provide no filtering though—the harmonic content of the output signal is changed by distorting the output of a DCO.

Decay
This is the second phase of the standard ADSR envelope shape. It is the rate at which the signal level falls from its peak value to the sustain level.

Decibel
The loudness of sounds is usually measured on a decibel scale. However, decibels can be used in other ways, such as expressing the losses through a filter. Decibels utilize a logarithmic scale.

Delay
In a synthesizer context this often refers to a facility that permits the modulation provided by the low frequency oscillator to be held-off for a preset period of time. It can also mean a type of circuit that delays an audio signal. These delaylines form the basis of many types of effects units, including chorus and reverberation.

Digital
See analogue.

Digital-to-analogue converter
See analogue-to-digital converter.

Drift
This is a problem that used to plague analogue synthesizers, but it is quite rare in modern digital instruments. It is where any setting of an instrument gradually shifts itself away from the setting you gave it. In particular, it refers to the drift in tuning which afflicts some synthesizers.

Droop
This is another problem that was not uncommon with analogue synthesizers, but which is not often encountered now. The sample and hold circuits in the keyboards of some instruments do not hold the keyboard voltage as well as they might. This usually manifests itself as a slight fall in pitch on notes which have a long release period.

Duty cycle
This term is applied to pulse signals, and it is a measure of the positive period compared to the total length of the pulse. A 10% duty cycle would give a short positive pulse—a 50% duty cycle would be a perfect squarewave.

Dynamics
The dynamics of a sound are its changes in volume.

Echo
An echo effect can be obtained by repeating a sound and gradually decreasing its volume on each repetition. There are units that will take in any signal and process it to produce an echo effect. With synthesizers this may not be necessary, and the modulation section of the instrument might be able to give a good pseudo-echo effect.

Ensemble
See chorus.

Envelope
The way in which the volume of a sound changes over a period of time, or (more accurately) a control voltage used to drive a VCA and give the required variations in volume to the processed signal.

Envelope generator
The device that generates an envelope voltage. Together with a VCA it forms an envelope shaper.

Equal temperament
A system of musical scaling which has the same pitch ratio for any two adjacent notes. This is the scale used in most (probably all) synthesizers, and many acoustic instruments as well come to that.

Expander
An instrument that has no keyboard or other built-in method of

148

playing it. Units of this type are usually controlled from a keyboard or a computer via a MIDI link.

Factory preset
As programming many modern synthesizers is something more than child's play, most synthesizers have a range of ready-programmed sounds available. They can therefore be used by anyone, even if they have little understanding of the instrument. Only using the factory presets means severely under-utilizing most instruments though.

Feedback
Taking the output of any electronic circuit and connecting it back to its input is a form of feedback. Normally only a small amount of signal is fed back to the input of the circuit. Resonance in a filter is obtained by using a controlled amount of feedback.

Filter
An electronic circuit that enables some frequencies to pass normally but attenuates others. Tone controls on a hi-fi amplifier are a simple form of filter.

FM synthesis
A method of synthesis that utilizes one sinewave generator to frequency modulate another, thus giving a complex output signal.

Frequency
The pitch of a signal expressed as a frequency in hertz (Hz) rather than as a musical note. Middle A is at 440Hz, which means that there are 440 complete cycles in one second.

Frequency modulation
This means using the output from a circuit to vary the pitch of a voltage controlled oscillator. In addition to FM synthesis, this is also used to provide vibrato in any synthesizer.

Fundamental
Repetitive waveforms consists of a fundamental signal plus certain harmonics (signals at multiples of the fundamental frequency). An instrument producing middle A at 440Hz therefore has a fundamental frequency of 440Hz, but would probably be producing harmonics at some multiples of this frequency (perhaps the second harmonic at 880Hz and the fourth at 1760Hz).

Gain
The amplitude ratio of an output signal to an input signal. Decibels are often used for gain measurements (negative values indicating a drop in signal level).

Glide
Rather than having an instant change from one note to the next, most synthesizers permit the pitch to change at a relatively slow rate from one note to the next. This is also known as 'portamento'.

Glitch
This is a general term which describes a momentary fault in an electronic circuit.

Harmonic
See fundamental.

Hertz (Hz)
The unit in which frequency is measured. A frequency of 1 hertz means there is one complete cycle per second. High audio frequencies are usually expressed in kilohertz (kHz). One kilohertz is equal to 1000 hertz.

Highpass filter
This is a filter that permits high frequencies to pass, but which attenuates frequencies below its cutoff frequency. This has the effect of attenuating the fundamental and (possibly) the lower harmonics, giving a thin and buzzy sound.

Keyboard priority
If you play more notes at once than an instrument can provide, the instrument has to decide which notes to miss out. The most common type of keyboard priority is probably the last note type, where the last note is always played, and usually the note that has been playing the longest is terminated in order to make way for it. A lot of monophonic analogue synthesizers have highest note priority. However many keys you hold down, only the note dictated by the highest key will be produced. With some instruments you can select one from a number of priority options.

LA
LA (linear arithmetic) synthesis is an odd but very effective mixture of sampled sounds and conventional analogue synthesis techni-

ques. The system used in a number of Roland's more recent synthesizers.

Last note priority
See keyboard priority.

Layering
Also known as stacking, this is where two or more voices of an instrument can be played with each key-press. Some very complex sounds can be obtained by layering a multi-timbral instrument, or using several interconnected instruments to obtain the same result.

LFO
This stands for 'low frequency oscillator'. In this context low frequency means in the region of 0.1 to about 10 or 20Hz. An LFO is used for modulation purposes—its output is too low in pitch to be audible.

Linear arithmetic
See LA.

Looping
The process of using the end section of a sample over and over again, so that rather than coming to an abrupt end, the signal is sustained indefinitely. Conventional envelope shaper techniques are normally used to give the signal the desired release characteristic.

Lowpass filter
This is a filter which lets signals below the cutoff frequency pass unattenuated, but which attenuates signals at frequencies above the cutoff frequency. This is the standard form of filter in analogue synthesizers, and pseudo-analogue synthesizers. In many cases this is the only form of filtering available.

MIDI
MIDI stands for 'musical instrument digital interface'. It is a means of controlling one instrument from another, or controlling an instrument from a computer. MIDI is a very versatile and capable system of interfacing suitably equipped musical instruments (see *Practical MIDI Handbook* for a full explanation of MIDI).

Modifier
Any device which acts on and alters a signal in some way.

Modular
In the early days of synthesizers a lot of these instruments were built from modules. You built up an instrument by obtaining a keyboard and case and then adding as many VCO modules, VCA modules, etc. as you required (or could afford). Everything was usually connected together with patch leads, enabling an assortment of modulation possibilities. It is a very versatile way of doing things, but is impracticable with the complexities of modern instruments.

Modulator
In FM synthesis an operator that frequency modulates another operator is called a modulator. In fact any signal source that provides modulation of another signal could be termed a modulator. So could any device that provides some special form of modulation, such as a ring modulator.

Mod-wheel
A modulation wheel is present on most synthesizers. It is usually a large edge-type rotary control that is used to adjust the modulation depth provided by the LFO.

Monochord
With multi-oscillator synthesizers it is usually possible to offset the tuning of the oscillators by anything up to at least one octave. You can therefore play two or three different oscillators at once, with each one on a different note, even if the instrument is monophonic. The catch is that the musical interval between the oscillators is always the same whatever note you play, but this can still give a greatly enhanced sound, especially with a monophonic instrument.

Noise generator
A circuit that generates a noise (hissing) sound. This is useful to augment the signal produced by ordinary oscillators, and some sounds (rain, handclaps, etc.) can be produced using noise as the sole signal source. White noise is the standard (fairly high pitched) hissing sound, and pink noise is a filtered noise that has a more gentle sound, similar to steady rain falling.

Notch filter
This is a filter that permits most frequencies to pass unhindered, but which provides a very high level of attenuation over a narrow band of frequencies. This type of filter is not used a great deal in

sound synthesis, and is only available on very few synthesizers. Sweeping a notch filter having multiple notches gives the phasing effect.

Operator
The basic building block used in FM synthesis. It consists of a sinewave generator having a frequency control input, a VCA and an envelope generator.

Oscillator
An oscillator is the electronic equivalent of the resonator (such as a reed) in an acoustic instrument. It generates a signal of the required waveform, although only some simple wave shapes (triangle, sine, square, etc.) are easily generated. Complex waveforms are generated using several oscillators plus (possibly) filtering, or using a DCO.

Overtone
A term which is often used as an alternative to harmonic (but strictly speaking not quite the same).

Pan pot
The outputs of monophonic instruments can be mixed to produce a good stereo signal. A pan potentiometer (or just pan pot as it is better known) is a control that enables a monophonic signal to be positioned at any desired position in the stereo sound field.

Parameter
Anything on a synthesizer that can be adjusted (envelope rates and levels, filter frequencies, etc.) is a parameter.

Partial
One meaning of this word is to describe the individual frequency components in a signal. In Roland's LA synthesis terminology it means a basic sound (either sampled or a conventional synthesizer sound).

Patch
A patch is a method of interconnecting the various parts of a synth. It dates back to the modular synthesizer days when the instrument was wired up in the required manner using patch leads which connected to sockets on the front panel of the instrument.

Periodic
A term used to describe certain types of waveform. The essential feature of a periodic waveform is that it is repetitive, and it therefore has a definite pitch. Sine, triangular and sawtooth waveforms are all examples of periodic waveforms.

Phase
This is a term that is mostly used when describing one waveform's relationship to another. A complete cycle has the wave going through 360 degrees (180 degrees on the first half cycle, and then 180 degrees in the opposite direction on the second one). If one wave is half a cycle behind another one, it would therefore be said to be phase lagging it by 180 degrees.

Phase distortion
A method of synthesis that seems to be very similar to conventional analogue synthesis as far as the user is concerned. In fact there are no filters, and distortion of the signal generated by a DCO is used to give a signal having a controllable harmonic content. There are no VCFs or DCFs, but the DCW section of the instrument has much the same effect on the sound as one of these.

Pink noise
This is a hissing type noise sound, but it is lower in pitch than the standard white variety. Pink noise is normally generated by filtering white noise.

Pitch envelope
Some synthesizers have an envelope generator that can be used to vary the pitch of an instrument. This is a useful feature, as some acoustic instruments have some variation in their pitch during the course of each note. Some interesting effects can be produced using a feature of this type.

Portamento
See glide.

Preset
A term that can be applied to any set of parameters that are preprogrammed and can be quickly called up when needed. It normally describes a set of parameters that give a certain sound. The required sound can be selected by pushing a button or two,

and with most synthesizers there are dozens of presets loaded and available almost instantly.

Pressure sensitive
Touch sensitive keyboards generally use the speed with which a key is depressed to control the peak volume on the attack phase of the envelope. A pressure sensitive type will also use the key pressure to control the volume after the attack phase (usually on the sustain phase). The key pressure may also be used to control other parameters, particularly those of the VCF (or equivalent circuit).

Program
This is a term which has several meanings, but in a synthesizer context it normally refers to a set of sound data. In other words it is much the same as a preset.

Pulse
A pulse waveform is generally accepted as one where the signal is either at a high negative level, or a high positive one, and it switches rapidly from one to the other. A squarewave is a form of pulse signal, but a triangular wave, due to its gradual change from one peak level to the other, is not. Any brief and intermittent waveform tends to be called a pulse signal, regardless of its exact shape.

Pulse width modulation
The width of a synthesizer's pulse signal can often be controlled by a low frequency oscillator. As the LFO voltage increases and decreases, so does the width of the pulse signal. This varies the strength of the fundamental and low order harmonics, giving an effect that is similar to swept lowpass filtering.

Q
In a synthesizer context the term 'Q' is mainly used as an alternative to resonance.

Quickdisk
This is a disk of a similar type to those used to store computer data. However, at 2.8 inches in diameter a quickdisk does not conform to any computer standard, and these disks only seem to be used with samplers. Most samplers now seem to use standard 3.5 inch computer disks which are cheaper, tougher and have a much

higher capacity. This second point is important with the large memory capacities of many modern samplers. It can take both sides of several quickdisks to fully load a sampler with even quite modest amounts of memory.

RAM

This is the type of memory used in samplers to store the sample data. The electronics in the system can write data into this 'random access memory', unlike ROM (read only memory) which must be programmed at the manufacturing stage. ROM retains its contents indefinitely, but RAM loses the data it contains when the power is switched off. Disks are used to magnetically store samples where long-term storage is required (which it normally will be). Small amounts of RAM can be battery-backed. This means having a battery which maintains power to the RAM when the unit is switched off. The battery typically lasts about five years. Many synthesizers hold data for their preset sounds in RAM, and use this system of battery back-up.

Ramp waveform

Also known as a 'sawtooth' waveform, this is one where the wave steadily rises, and then almost instantly drops back to its original level. Alternatively, it can start at a high level, steadily drop, and then almost instantly jump back to its original level. These are ramp-up and ramp-down waveforms respectively. This waveform has a strong harmonic content, and is often used for brass and string type sounds.

Ratio tuning

This is the method of tuning used in most additive and FM synthesizers. The frequencies of the oscillators are given as a ratio relative to the fundamental frequency. A ratio of 3 would therefore be used to select the third harmonic.

Release

This is the final phase of the standard ADSR envelope generator. It controls how long a sound takes to die away after the key is released.

Resonance

VCFs almost invariably have a resonance control. When advanced, this produces a peak in the filter's response close to the cutoff frequency (or the centre frequency in the case of a bandpass filter).

For a notch filter things are a little different, and the effect of resonance is to narrow the width of the notch. Too much resonance will usually result in the filter breaking into oscillation ('ringing'). A lot of synth sounds rely on a swept VCF having a moderate to high resonance setting.

Reverberation
If a sound stops instantly at source, it will usually take a short while before the sound you hear decays to an inaudible level. This is due to sounds reflecting around the walls, floor, ceiling, etc., and reaching the listener via indirect routes. These routes are longer than the direct one, and the sound takes longer to arrive. This is known as reverberation, and in a large hall it can take as much as a few seconds for the reverberation to subside. A reverberation unit electronically mimics this effect, so that an electronically generated signal can be given the big hall sound. In fact most reverberation effects units now offer a range of room sizes.

Ringing
See resonance.

Ring modulator
A ring modulator combines the output of two oscillators to produce sum and difference frequencies. It is mainly used in the production of metallic sounds such as bells and gongs. A small amount of ring modulated sound can enhance other types of sound though.

Roll-off
This is the common term for the attenuation rate of a filter. A filter which has a fast roll-off is one which will severely attenuate signals even if they are as little as an octave beyond the cutoff frequency.

ROM
Read only memory (see RAM).

Sample and hold
The keyboard circuit of an analogue synthesizer uses a sample and hold circuit to maintain the last keyboard voltage when a key is released. Sample and hold circuits can also be used with a low frequency oscillator and a noise generator to produce an output at a frequency determined by the LFO, but with a random amplitude.

This signal can be used to provide modulation having a frequency set by the LFO, but random depth.

Sampling
This is a form of digital recording and playback. Sounds are recorded into the instrument and stored in RAM. They are then played back at the desired pitch. This gives some very convincing acoustic instrument sounds, but a lot of weird and wonderful sounds can also be produced by sampling non-instrument sounds. Many samplers have complex VCFs, VCAs, envelope generators, LFOs and modulation sections, etc. This gives plenty of scope for modifying recorded sounds, and most samplers are considerably more than just recording and playback devices.

Sawtooth
See ramp waveform.

Sinewave
This is the most basic of waveforms in that it has only one component frequency (the fundamental). It has an unmistakably pure sound.

Subtractive synthesis
Subtractive synthesis is the standard analogue synthesizer method of sound synthesis. It is subtractive in that you must start with a signal that has all the harmonics the desired sound needs, and they must all be of adequate strength. Filtering is then used to trim back any excessively strong harmonics so as to give the required waveform.

Sustain
The sustain phase of an ADSR envelope generator differs from the others in that the user specifies a signal level rather than a rate of change. This phase lasts from the end of the decay stage until the key is released.

Sustain pedal
Many synthesizers have a socket for a sustain pedal. This gives an effect which is similar to that of a piano's sustain pedal. Notes have an extended release period, unless the instrument runs out of voices that is. Existing notes are then normally terminated to make way for the new ones.

Timbre

The characteristics of sounds that distinguish one instrument from another. Timbre is mainly governed by the harmonic content and envelope of a signal. It is these differences in timbre that result in one instrument sounding very different from another playing the same note.

Time variant amplifier

This is much the same as an envelope shaper.

Time variant filter

Essentially just a modern term for a VCF plus envelope generator.

Touch sensitive

This applies to a keyboard that provides velocity information to the synthesizer. This information is normally used to control the volume of each note, so that playing the keyboard hard gives increased volume. The velocity information often controls the filtering as well. A good touch sensitive keyboard will also implement aftertouch.

Tremolo

An effect which is obtained by using a low frequency oscillator to amplitude modulate the output of an instrument.

Triangle waveform

A waveform that rises at a steady rate, and then falls at the same rate. This waveform has a low harmonic content, and is only suitable for synthesizing instruments such as flutes which do not have bright sounds.

VCA

A voltage controlled amplifier (VCA) is one of the basic building blocks of a synthesizer. By varying the control voltage, the amplitude of the output signal varies in a corresponding manner. Together with an envelope generator, a VCA forms an envelope shaper.

VCF

A voltage controlled filter (VCF) is another basic building block for synthesizers. The cutoff frequency of the filter is controlled by an input voltage. This control voltage is normally derived from a frequency control, the keyboard, and an envelope generator. The

VCF is crucial to subtractive synthesis. The varying cutoff frequency of the filter provides changes in the waveform during the course of each note.

VCO
Yet another basic synth building block, the voltage controlled oscillator (VCO) is the circuit that generates the basic sound. This is then modified by the VCA and VCF to mould the sound and give precisely the desired effect. Many synthesizers have two or more VCOs which can be used together to give much richer sounds.

Vocoder
A vocoder is an effects unit, and although they were all the rage at one time, they seem to be little used these days. One incoming signal is used to control a bank of filters that process a second signal. This has the effect of imposing some characteristics of one signal on the second. The main use of a vocoder is to make a synthesizer or other electronic instrument 'sing', by controlling it from a voice signal.

Voltage control
It is voltage control that largely distinguishes synthesizers from other instruments. The main point about having everything, as far as possible, under voltage control, is that it enables virtually any part of the instrument to control virtually any other part. This permits complex modulation to be used, and equally complex sounds to be generated.

White noise
White noise is the standard high pitched hissing noise sound.

Appendix 2: Useful addresses

Magazines (UK)

Home Keyboard Review, Alexander House, 1 Milton Road, Cambridge CB4 1UY

International Musician, Cover Publications, Northern & Shell Building, PO Box 381, Mill Harbour, London E14 9TW

Music Technology, Alexander House, 1 Milton Road, Cambridge CB4 1UY

Sound on Sound, The Coach House, 9b The Broadway, St Ives, Cambridgeshire PE17 4BX

What Keyboard?, Cover Publications, Northern & Shell Building, PO Box 381, Mill Harbour, London E14 9TW

Manufacturers (UK)

Akai, Electronic Music Division, Haslemere Heathrow Estate, Silver Jubilee Way, Parkway, Hounslow, Middx TW4 6NQ (Tel 01-897 6388)

Casio Electronic Co Limited, Unit 6, 1000 North Circular Road, London NW2 7JD (Tel 01-450 9131)

Electromusic Research, 14 Mount Close, Wickford, Essex SS11 8HG (Tel 0702 335747)

Elka-Orla UK, 3/5 Fourth Avenue, Bluebridge Ind Estate, Halstead, Essex CO9 2SY (Tel 0787 475325)

Emu Systems, Syco, Conduit Place, London W2 (Tel 01-724 2451)

Ensoniq UK, PO Box 806, London NW3 1HZ (Tel 01-435 2434)

Farfisa UK, Fraser Street, Burnley, Lancs BB1 1UL (Tel 0282 35431)

John Hornby Skewes, Salem House, Garforth, Leeds LS25 1PX (Tel 0532 865381)

Kawai UK, Windebank House, 2 Durley Road, Bournemouth BH2 5JJ (Tel 0202 296629)

Korg UK, 8–9 The Crystal Centre, Elm Grove Road, Harrow, Middx HA1 2YR (Tel 01-427 5377)

Oberheim, 6 Letchworth Business Centre, Avenue 1, Letchworth, Herts SG6 2HR (Tel 0462 480000)

Roland (UK) Limited, Great West Trading Estate, 983 Great West Road, Brentford, Middx (Tel 01-568 4578)

Rosetti, 138 Old Street, London EC1V 9BL

Sequential Inc, PO Box 16, 3640 AA Mijdtrecht, The Netherlands

Simmons, Alban Park, Hatfield Road, St Albans, Herts AL4 0JH

Steinberg Research, The Studio, Church Street, Stonesfield, Oxford OX7 2PS (Tel 099389 228)

Technics, 300 Bath Road, Slough, Berks SL1 6JB (Tel 0753 34522)

Yamaha, Mount Avenue, Bletchley, Milton Keynes, Bucks MK1 1JE (Tel 0908 71771)

Other organizations (UK)

Akai Active, Haslemere Heathrow Estate, Silver Jubilee Way, Parkway, Hounslow, Middx TW4 6NQ (Tel 01-897 6388)

Casio MIDI User's Club, Unit 6, 1000 North Circular Road, London NW2 7JD (Tel 01-450 9131)

Mirage User Group, 2 Walnut Tree Cottages, The Green, Frant, E Sussex TN3 9DE

Roland Newslink, Roland (UK), Great West Trading Estate, 983 Great West Road, Brentford, Middx (Tel 01-568 4578)

Steinberg User Club, 68 Wilsdon Way, Kidlington, Oxford OX5 1TX

Yamaha X Club, Mount Avenue, Bletchley, Milton Keynes, Bucks MK1 1JE (Tel 0908 78894)

Magazines (USA and Canada)

Canadian Musician, 832 Mount Pleasant Road, Toronto, Ontario, M4P 2L3

Electronic Musician Magazine, 2608 Ninth Street, Berkeley, CA 94710

International Musician, Suite 600, Paramount Building, 1501 Broadway, NY 10036

Keyboard, 20085 Stevens Creek, Cupertino, CA 95014

Mix Magazine, 2608 Ninth Street, Berkeley, CA 94710

Modern Drummer, 870 Pompton Avenue, Cedar Grove, New Jersey 07009

Music, Computers and Software, 190 East Main Street, Huntingdon, NY

Music & Sound Output, 25 Willowdale Ave, Port Washington, NY 11050

Music Technology, 7361 Topanga Canyon Blvd., Canoga Park, CA 91303

Musician, 1515 Broadway, 39th Floor, NY 10036

Percussion, 6 Avenue J, Brooklyn, NY 11230

Manufacturers (USA)

Akai Professional, PO Box 2344, Fort Worth, Texas, TX76113

Alesis, PO Box 3908, Los Angeles, CA 90078

Casio, 15 Gardner Road, Fairfield, NJ 07006

EMU Systems, 1600 Green Hills Road, Scotts Valley, CA 95066

Ensoniq, 155 Great Valley Parkway, Malvern, PA 19355

Fairlight, 2945 Westwood Blvd., Los Angeles, CA 90064

Fostex, 15431 Blackburn Ave, Norwalk, CA 90650

Kawai America, 2055 East University Drive, PO Box 9045, Compton, CA 90224

Korg USA, 89 Frost Street, Westbury, NY 11590

Kurzweil Music Systems, 411 Waverley Oaks Road, Waltham, MA 02154

Oberheim, 11650 W Olympic Blvd, Los Angeles, CA 90064

Roland Corp US, 7200 Dominion Circle, Los Angeles, CA 90040

Sequential Circuits Inc, 3051 North First Street, San Jose, CA 95134

Simmons USA, 23917 Craftsman Road, Calabasas, CA 91302

Yamaha, PO Box 6600, Buena Park, CA 90622

Other organizations (USA)

International MIDI Association, 11857 Hartsook Street, North Hollywood, CA 91607

MIDI Manufacturers' Association, c/o Roland Corp US, 7200 Dominion Circle, Los Angeles, CA 90040

Roland User Group, c/o Roland Corp US, 7200 Dominion Circle, Los Angeles, CA 90040

Index

Your best accessory!

Make money from

HOME RECORDING

CLIVE BROOKS

110 pages · 216 × 138 mm
10 illustrations
ISBN: 1 870775 25 2
£5.95

★ For recording enthusiasts and musicians

★ Cover price recouped as soon as the first idea is put into practice

★ All ideas tried and tested by the author

★ Written in jargon-free style

★ Lists of useful addresses

Now that you've spent a fortune on all that recording gear, MIDI and all, wouldn't it be nice to get some of it back? Well here's the book to show you how.

It's packed with money-making ideas, anyone of which will recoup the price of the book many times over. Whether you have a fully fledged recording studio at home, or just a couple of stereo cassette recorders and a microphone, you'll be able to put the ideas in this book into practice and make money.

Clive Brooks also covers all the other things you'll need to know, like advertising and selling your products, keeping track of finances, and insurance. There are also some useful names and addresses at the back of the book to put you in touch with magazines, manufacturers, tape duplicating companies etc.

Contents
Introduction. Setting up a studio. Studio equipment. Moneymaking ideas. How to sell your services. A guide to good publicity. Hiring out your studio. The business background. The end of the beginning. Appendix. Useful addresses. Index.

Send a cheque or postal order for £6.45 (£5.95 plus 50p P&P) made payable to PC Publishing, to PC Publishing, 4 Brook Street, Tonbridge, Kent TN9 2PJ